REDLINE ARCHEOLOGY II
The Dig Continues....

Bonus Feature:
A Collector's GUIDE to Finding REDLINE Hot Wheels Collections

Author: Bob Young, Chief Redline Archeologist

Hot Wheels, Redline, Spectraflame, Sizzlers, Flying Colors, and all associated trademarks are registered and owned by Mattel, Incorporated and are used in this book solely for identification purposes. Neither the author nor the publisher of this book are sponsored by or associated with Mattel, Incorporated. The cars, race sets, and accessories featured and photographed in this book are from the Bob Young personal collection and owned exclusively by Bob Young. All rights reserved.

The information within this book is true and complete to the best of the author's knowledge. Any and all recommendations are made without any guarantee on the part of the author or publisher, who disclaim any liability incurred in connection with the use of the information or any specific details.

Copyright 2021 Bob Young
All rights reserved

ISBN -978-0-578-95301-4

REDLINE ARCHEOLOGY II
The Dig Continues....

Bonus Feature:
A Collector's GUIDE to Finding REDLINE Hot Wheels Collections

Author: Bob Young, Chief Redline Archeologist

REDLINE ARCHEOLOGY II
"The DIG Continues"
A Collector's Guide to Discovering Hot Wheels Collections

Table of Contents

Acknowledgments 7
Introduction... 9

Chapter I	The Moment 13	
Chapter II	Most Amazing Toy Car in the World............................ 17	
Chapter III	My Approach to Collecting.. 21	
Chapter IV	The Appraisal Process... 23	
Chapter V	Making the Offer.. 32	
Chapter VI	Finalizing the Deal.. 34	
Chapter VII	"How To" Guide to Collecting....................................... 37	
	1. Grass Roots Approach................................ 39	
	2. The Business Card..................................... 40	
	3. Flyers... 42	
	4. The No Cost Publication........................... 45	
	5. The Local Media Outlets........................... 46	
	6. The World Wide Web................................ 47	
	7. Today's Internet.. 49	
	8. The BLOG... 51	
	9. The YOUTUBE Channel........................... 53	
	10. Facebook... 54	
	11. Additional Options.................................... 56	
	12. The JOBBY.. 57	
	13. Overview... 58	
	14. The Archeological Assets......................... 59	
Chapter VIII	My Most Recent Discoveries... 61	
	1. Corona, California Collection.......................... 62	
	2. South Philly Collection.................................... 68	
	3. El Dorado Hills, California Collection............ 79	
	4. Arlington, Virginia Collection......................... 85	
	5. San Luis Obispo, California Collection.......... 90	
	6. British Columbia, Canada Collection............. 96	
	7. Sacramento, California Collection................. 101	
	8. Lodi, California Collection............................. 107	
	9. Red Oak, Iowa Collection............................... 113	
	10. El Paso, Texas Collection............................... 124	
	11. Circlesville, Ohio Collection........................... 128	
	12. Kamuela, Hawaii Collection.......................... 134	
	13. Wildwood, Missouri Collection...................... 138	
	14. Sothern New Jersey Collection...................... 142	
	15. Blue Anchor, New Jersey Collection.............. 147	
	16. Northglenn, Colorado Collection................... 153	
	17. Lunenberg, Massachusetts Collection........... 163	
Chapter IX	Final Tally... 168	
Chapter X	BEST of the BEST Discoveries...................................... 171	
Chapter XI	REDLINE ARCHEOLOGY Personal Collection............ 174	
Chapter XII	The Beginning.. 179	

ACKNOWLEDGEMENTS

First and foremost, I must give all the credit for my passion of the original Hot Wheels and the love of cars in general to my parents, George, and Betty. If it were not for them buying me my first Custom Camaro and Strip Action Set back on July 1, 1968, not sure if you would be reading this book right now. It started me on a journey that was paused in 1972 when I discovered girls and reignited in 1992 when my mother told me to get mine and my brother's old toys out of the attic.

Next, I must recognize my beautiful wife and all her unfettered support of all my craziness surrounding this wonderful and unique hobby of mine. She has never wavered once and continues to smile every time a new collection arrives from around the world. I think she is finally getting it. 😉

Moving on to my three amazing and beautiful kids, Madison, Kyle, and Natalie for always getting a kick out of what I do. It amuses me, watching their expressions when I start talking passionately about my Hot Wheels. They all seem to let out a collective chuckle when I get going. Now who did I say I am leaving my cars to?

I would be remiss if I did not acknowledge my good friend and fellow collector, Todd Deschaine. I have met some great people in the hobby over the years, but he stands out head and shoulders above the rest. Todd and I have spent hours on end talking about our love of the Redline Era Hot Wheels and he always seemed to be there to share in the excitement of all the collections I would dig up. We really shared some great moments and times together and I will always cherish those memories. In addition, he is credited for most of the pictures in my first book: **"Redline Archeology "A History of Diggin' Up Original Hot Wheels Collections"**... By the way, I am still trying to get this guy back in the hobby.

Next up is my wonderful mother-in-law, Joyka. Her real name is Joyce, but I know her as Joyka. Thanks for always supporting me, not only in this hobby, but all along my lifelong journey with all my crazy business ideas and ventures. I think she would tell you that I am the most interesting person in the family 😉 and that is probably the understatement of the century.

Finally, my good pal Larry Siegel who has stood by me and all my crazy ideas for the past twenty years. Fortunately, or unfortunately, we share the same distorted sense of humor. Larry is the true consummate professional and I do give credit for a chunk of my success to him. My dear friend Larry, thanks for always being there!

INTRODUCTION

My love of Hot Wheels began on Friday, July 1st, 1968. I remember the day like it was yesterday. It was my eighth birthday party and I could not have been more excited to celebrate it with all my best of friends. The memories for me remain in full color and high definition. It was a day that had such an impact on my young life, that I recall almost every aspect of it, even all those that were in attendance. I can even tell you the time of day and place. The magic day had its beginnings at the Stratford Swim Club, in a small town called Stratford, NJ just outside of Philadelphia, PA and about an hour from the Jersey Shore. We finally arrived at the swim club and me and my band of hyper-active buddies were fighting to exit my parent's four door, 1964 Chevrolet Bel-Air. It is a wonder one of us did not end up in the emergency room that day the way we were battling to exit the car. Hands were put in each other's faces with a gentle shove; well maybe not so gentle. Afterall, we were Jersey Boys. We finally fell out of the car onto the dirt parking lot and scrambled to see who could make it to the front desk first. Back then you had to check in and sign in prior to entering the swim club and boy were they strict about that unyielding rule. One by one, the pen was tossed or thrown at or to each other and we slowly wrote out our names. It felt like time stood still as a couple of my friends did not have the best penmanship. Looking back, a few of them stuck out their tongues like Michael Jordan and leaned into the ledger with their heads tilted at forty-five degrees while laboring through the signature process. We had not learned cursive at that point, so each letter was painstakingly written. Trust me, if we had YOUTUBE back then, we all would have cashed in on the video. Like missiles being shot, one after another, we fired out of the main lobby in a b-line to the picnic table area just past the large Olympic-sized pool and under the large oak trees. The absolute hilarious part, other than just about everything leading up to this point, was that the entire time we were sprinting to get to the decorated birthday picnic table, every lifeguard in the place was either blowing their whistle at us or screaming for us to stop running. Running around the pool was a real "NO NO" and could get you benched for thirty minutes, which was nothing short of a lifetime for us seven and eight year-olds. Times were so different back then but looking back, it was truly the best of times. Just thinking about that day still makes me laugh out loud a bit.

All my best friends were there, sitting at the exquisitely decorated picnic table in my honor. It was approximately 12 noon EST, and the temperature was in the upper 70's. There had even been a brief thunderstorm that day, but it did not hinder or ruin one moment of my incredible day. Yes, crazy as it sounds, we even stood under large trees until the storm passed. Our parents actually told us to. The Stratford Swim Club was ground zero for local kids' birthday parties, cooling off, and just having some fun in the sun back in the day. Every Stratford kid wanted to have their birthday party there. I was just lucky and fortunate enough to have my eighth birthday there. Very few people in Stratford had a pool in their backyards, and the ones that did were typically above ground. We knew where every pool was in town, and by the time my friends and I became young teenagers, we were "pool hopping" on a regular basis during our summer vacations from school. Pool hopping was a real thing back then, kind of like streaking, but we did keep our bathing suits on, and boy was it fun. However, not so much fun when you got caught and your parents were notified.

The Stratford Swim Club located in Stratford, NJ

As I have said, it was my eighth birthday, and the anticipation leading up to it almost made me pass out at times. I think I even crashed my bike into a neighbor's car at one point daydreaming about it one day. I was raised in this blue-collar town, by my father who was a decorated World War II Veteran and Texaco Oil refinery worker, and my mother who was a Personnel Specialist for the JC Penney, Co. in Audubon, New Jersey. We were certainly afforded all the freedom of the times, like leaving the house in the morning during the summertime, and only coming back home to eat and occasionally use the facilities, if you get my drift. We played all day, every day, rain, or shine. We would play stickball for hours on end, street hockey until either our legs fell off or a bench clearing brawl would break out, or we knew our parents would be calling us in for dinner. We ran through the woods, built makeshift forts, and would even fish at the local sewerage plant. The Stratford Sewer plant stunk to high heaven, but it was a great place to catch carp, sunfish, and catfish which were known for putting up the biggest fight. My mother would not let me in the house until I stripped my dirty fishing clothes off in the garage and then took a shower. I can only imagine what I smelled like after eight hours of fishing at the local sewerage plant. She would even pack me a brown paper bag lunch with a peanut butter sandwich, the crust cut off of course, and some peanut butter Tandy Takes. Looking back, it probably was one of the most impactful things for strengthening my immune system. After hours of digging for worms, setting the bait, and catching fish, I would grab that sandwich and Tandy Takes out of their wrappers and eat them with my bare, dirty, wormy, fishy hands. Grotesque I know, but we were also the generation that would close our lips, one after another, around a garden hose in the summertime to rehydrate and cool down. Things that were normal back then seem very abnormal now, but it was just how things were back in the sixties and seventies.

Street hockey was one of mine and my friends' favorite past times and we would play for hours on end. Sometimes while playing street hockey, we would start a fight just to end a game if we wanted to move onto something else, or we knew that our parents screeching (moms) or booming (dads) voices would be calling us in for dinner in the next few moments from our respective front porches. Our parents would always give us the "stink eye" if we stayed in the house for what they perceived as too long. Yes, it's all true what they say... We were to be seen, but not that much, and not heard unless spoken to. It was a vastly different time as I have said back in the sixties and seventies, but what a glorious time it was. A childhood that I occasionally reflect on, and tell lots of stories about, to my kids, friends, family, and sometimes even complete strangers. Yes, we drank from garden hoses to hydrate our emaciated and sweaty summer bodies. Yes, we even had fights with our friends, and then shook hands at the end, and all was well in paradise once again. Yes, we did not ever check in with our parents during the day and were gone sometimes for 12-hour clips. Surprisingly, nor did our parents ever come looking for us. I guess they knew we were coming back at some time, and we always did. Yes, we had rock and crab apple fights, and even would drip honeysuckle on our tongues from the flowering plants that lined the fence where our stickball games took place. It was truly a magical and amazing childhood, and I would not trade a second of it for anything in the world. Not even a Rear Loader Beach Bomb.

There we were, Paul, Bobby C., Jeff, Joe, Timmy, and John all seated at the picnic table waiting for our hot dog and potato chip lunch, anticipating the cake. All our skinny little legs were going a mile a minute under the table, swinging back and forth burning a thousand calories an hour. Even when we sat still, there were many moving parts that were basically uncontrollable. We all had our eyes fixated and locked on that oh so delicious pile of confectioner's sugar and icing that stared back at us from the other side of the table. We could not eat our hot dogs fast enough, because we all knew that the cake was on deck just waiting to be devoured. I swear, to this day, that cake stuck its tongue out and gave me and all my friends a big raspberry. Well, that is what it felt like waiting for what seemed like an eternity to sink our teeth into that beautiful, scrumptious delight. That cake did not know what hit it. After collectively devouring that helpless vanilla cake, it was time to open all my presents. The moment had finally arrived. The sun broke through the clouds, trumpets from the heavens started to play, angels appeared, and all eyes were focused on me. My eyes, well they were fixed on that small pile of presents that my friends so graciously provided. Oh, the presents were like a gift sent from God to this eight-year-old. Presents from my friends were always so much better than the essential ones given to me by my parents, like a new JC Penney brand bathing suit, JC Penney socks, JC Penney t-shirts, and a pair of PF Flyers. PF Flyers were the poor boys' version of Converse Chuck Taylors, and yes, they were embarrassing to wear around town even in 1968. It was either wear the PF Flyers or go barefoot. I really did not have a choice, but I did have a plan. My parents also questioned me as to why my PF Flyers wore out so fast, especially the rubber soles on both shoes. I would always reiterate to my mother that they were so cheaply made as compared to my friends' Chuck Taylors. If I were only given the chance to own my own pair of Chuck Taylors, all would be good in this little boy's world. Well, even though my mother was not educated past twelfth grade, she was incredibly intuitive and intelligent. I was not confident that my plan would work but I had to give it the old Elementary School try. By the way, I never let the cat out of the bag until now. The brakes on my Schwinn bike worked perfectly fine but were rarely used. The PF Flyers provided all the stopping power I needed. It worked, and the rest is, as they say, history.

Well, my parents certainly did not disappoint on this special day either, but we will get to that later. I proceeded to open all my presents and my friends, of course, never disappointed. I received a large Superball, Johnny West Action Figure, a couple of board games, and a Captain Action figure. The life changing moment was still about 6 hours away at my home following dinner. Even my grandparents came over to celebrate their favorite grandson's birthday. Oh, come on now, of course I was their favorite and who would blame them, right? I remember them all and miss them every day. I do, however, have to give my mother and father all the credit for getting me started on this crazy and exciting, lifelong journey with my favorite toy car, Hot Wheels.

CHAPTER I

The MOMENT

The day of fun in the sun at the Stratford Swim Club was coming to an end, and we all packed up, piled into my friend Paul's family station wagon, and headed on the long one-mile journey home to Laurel Mills Farm and Hillcrest Road where most of us called home. We all sat on the drop-down tailgate door with our feet dangling inches above the street. This was a real treat for us neighborhood kids during the summertime. Our little legs were swaying back and forth, and in circles like eggbeaters, from the moment we planted ourselves onto our well fought over space on the tailgate, pushing and shoving our way for position until we were scolded to "knock it off." We tended to hear those three words quite frequently when we all got together. We squeezed tightly together so each of us could enjoy the excitement of watching the road quickly pass under our feet and the houses and street signs fly on by. It truly was an exciting thing for a little boy in the sixties. We all loved the one speed bump on the way home as it made us all literally suspend in the air for that one special and exhilarating split second. Boy did we all collectively scream in unison and laugh out loud when that happened. Something that I will never forget. Somehow, we all survived these times, even as crazy as it sounds today, as I look back on how profoundly different my childhood truly was.

Hillcrest Road, my childhood home where the journey began with Hot Wheels

It was late in the afternoon, and all the moms in the neighborhood were busily preparing dinner for all their hungry troops. There was no home delivery or take out back then. We ate exactly what our mothers prepared, and we were expected to clean our plates, even those obnoxious and utterly tasteless green beans that seemed to appear all too often. I think I personally missed out on ten percent of my childhood due to those inconvenient vegetables. My mother would stare at me endlessly until every lousy green bean passed my lips and dropped down my esophagus into my tiny stomach. I literally grimaced with every minuscule bite that I fought through, grunting, and complaining the entire time until, of course, I was told to "Knock it Off." We were also expected to ask each of our parents to be excused from the dinner table upon finishing our meal. Depending on my parents' mood, determined whether I was furloughed on the first request or had to sit there, on my hands, until either warden granted my request, which sometimes felt like an eternity. I usually exited under the table dodging everyone's legs and especially my brothers as he always tried to get that extra shot in on me any chance he got. This type of family structure and rules have all but vanished in our culture.

Laurel Mills Farm, my childhood neighborhood in Stratford, NJ

Let us get back to the "moment" that would ultimately have a huge and defining influence on my life, then and now. The table in the dining room was set for seven to accommodate my mother's parents. We were called to dinner precisely at six o'clock and we all sat down in our assigned seats. We basically knew the pecking order in the family over the years with my father at the head of the table to my left and my mother to the right. My grandfather, Pop-Pop Wendell, always sat to my left and would torture me during every dinner we had together. He would make me laugh like no other at the time. He is talked about more in my family to this day, and we all collectively laugh just as hard reminiscing, especially my cousins. Pop-Pop would always take out his full set of dentures when I was not looking and give me a big smile that I can still see clearly to this day, smacking his toothless lips and making a sound that always got me going. Of course, he and I got yelled at to "Knock it Off" if we carried it too far as we always seemed to do, but we just could not help ourselves. Sometimes I catch myself doing some of the same things he did to me to my kids and granddaughter Savannah, minus the denture skit of course. He would always tap me on my opposite shoulder, look away and act like I was crazy. I fell for it every time. He really enjoyed grabbing my left leg just above my knee and squeezing as hard as he could when of course, I had a mouth full of food. Well, I guess you can imagine where the chewed food ended up. I just wish his timing were better towards the end of my meal when it was green bean time. He was extraordinarily strong back in the day, at least that is what I thought anyway as I was writhing in pain trying to break free of the left knee death grip. At the same time, my loving and protective Mam-Mom was reaching for her wooden cane ready to strike him if he did not release his grip. He usually took a beating anyway, but I still, to this day, think that he thought it was all worth it to see me squirm. Like I said before, it was such a different time growing up in the sixties. I guess I loved the attention he gave me and do miss the crazy old man. On a side note, we both typically were asked to leave the dinner table, and most times we gladly obliged laughing all the way out of the dining room.

Dinner was served, and we all ate a hardy meal of roast beef, potatoes, and the dreaded peas. Peas always had a way of delaying my departure from the dinner table as well during my youth. I despised them as much as the green beans, and always had to choke down each one while my hawk of a mother witnessed every bite until they were gone. I would painfully eat a half of a pea at a time, wincing with every disgusting and revolting bite. Peas have never been on the menu in the Young household during the latter part of the twentieth century and certainly not during the twenty first century. I do not even think my three kids know what a pea looks like.

My grandmother was always the slowest eater in the family, but we all had to sit there and watch her finish her meal. She was always twenty to thirty minutes slower than the rest of us, even with peas on the table. We loved her dearly and really did not mind, except it was my birthday. I remember thinking, please Mam Mom, chew faster. I wanted to grab her head and jaw and help her chew faster, but I knew that would be the last thing I did on this earth if I even broached the subject. Well, after almost flipping the calendar, my grandmother finally finished her meal, and we were on to my second cake. The candles were lit, and the singing began. It was truly an incredibly special day in a Baby Boomers life in the sixties. A day that was almost as good as Christmas, almost. As an adult, I am not a fan of celebrating my birthday ever; there are just too many of them at this point. Birthday celebrations during my childhood were almost as good as Christmas. As soon as the singing ended, my grandmother planted her big, wet proverbial kiss on my left cheek, while wrestling my head in place so she could accomplish it. For some reason, I always tried to squirm away from any of my relative's kisses, but I would give anything to let her kiss my cheek today. I miss her immensely.

I blew out the massive amount of eight candles and turned and looked everyone at the table in the eye. My eyes were saying, let's go people, step up to the plate and deliver me a great present. The presents seemed to appear out of nowhere, one after the other, and it felt like it would never end. At least that is what I truly was hoping for. I, of course, was given the essentials first by my mother and there were no surprises. The PF Flyers, the new JC Penney brand bathing suit, socks, and a three pack of JC Penney t-shirts. I ripped through those four boxes quickly, paper and ribbons flying everywhere, in hopes of getting to the goods, toys, and more toys hopefully. Little did I know that my mother was in collusion with my grandmother in purchasing what would turn out to be the start of something bigger than life itself for this skinny, little eight-year-old.

The "moment" had arrived, and I can still see it clearly as day. My mother passed me this long skinny box. I really did not know what to think. We were always trying to figure out what our presents were prior to opening them, especially at Christmas time. My parents hid my presents well, incredibly well. For them to keep the presents hidden from these prying eyes was an accomplishment upon itself. Let us cut to the chase. I opened the present and there appeared a Strip Action Set from Mattel, Inc.. Never were my eyes bigger, looking over what I truly did not understand, but what I knew was greatness. I just sensed it was the beginning of something amazing in my life. The colors on the box, the artwork, and all the cars pictured, it just had to be something spectacular I thought. I had never seen anything like it up to this point. I was then handed another gem by my mother. It was the black roof, white interior Custom Camaro blister pack, and this was the beginning of a journey that would take me places, and present experiences I would have never imagined. Afterall, it was only a sixty-seven-cent toy car that I never thought in a million years would be worth any more than that. Little did I know or understand how impactful this day would be in my life, or the amount or sheer enjoyment this toy line would bring to me throughout my life. So, it begins....

The Strip Action Set and Blue Custom Camaro that started it All

CHAPTER 2

The Most AMAZING Toy in the World

The "Fastest Metal Cars in the World." Truer words have never been spoken in describing the greatest and most amazing toy car line ever produced. Mattel's marketing campaign was one of a kind for the times. The print ads, Saturday morning commercials, packaging, store promotions, store displays, and the unparalleled graphics on their packaging were quite frankly, stunning. The extraordinarily talented and masterful Otto Kuhni, who was Mattel's chosen artist for their Hot Wheels line packaging, was a genius in his own right. His artwork that graced every Hot Wheels blister pack, race set and accessory package, was certainly one of a kind and incredible. The box art, with all the colors, was something that caught every child's eye and absolutely put me into a trance every time it was in my sight lines. The pictures of the cars, the track set ups, the unbelievable accessories, and the cars that appeared to be moving on the boxes, are to this day, candy for the eyes and imaginations of any passionate Hot Wheels collector, young or old. As we say, they just don't make 'em like this anymore. Then, there was what was in the packaging.

The cars were so cool with their shiny and colorful paint, five spoke red line wheels, California custom hot rod designs, and their amazing suspension that allowed the cars to run forever down the signature orange track with all the loops, curves, and jumps. If this was not enough, add in the Super Charger, Rod Runner, and Tune-Up Tower, and now you have got a set-up that was unrivaled for the times and for years to come. I would stare at these little gems for hours and would sometimes even place the cars under my pillow at night so they would be near to me and safe from intruders. Do not ask me why I did this or what was going on in my head at this time in my life, but it certainly describes the impact that these toy cars had on me in 1968.

Prior to 1968, all we had to play with, as far as toy vehicles were concerned, were Tonka Toy trucks and Matchbox toy cars. Neither was as exciting to me or my friends on the block. In my neighborhood, both toy truck and car lines usually ended up in someone's sandbox to rust or to be buried in a sandy grave. They never kept our attention for long, nor did we ever race to anyone's house to specifically play with them. They just were not cool to this little guy or any of his friends. This lack of coolness is what, in my opinion, set the table for the greatest toy car line ever to be produced, Hot Wheels. Still, the Matchbox toy car line was a huge success in the fifties and early to mid-sixties, and one that would not be challenged until years later by Mattel.

Elliot and Ruth Handler, along with Harold "Matt" Matson were the founders of Mattel, Inc. back in 1945. The Handlers, would both, incredibly and unbelievably go on to create the greatest, most popular selling girl's and boy's toy lines, that even holds true to this day. Ruth was first responsible for the creation, production, and release of Barbie in 1959.What a huge success it was and continues to be over sixty-two years later and still going strong. Elliot Handler was also a visionary that wanted to capture a chunk of the diecast 1:64 toy car line that

Lesney of England had a stronghold on since 1953, when the first Matchbox cars were released to the public. Elliot wanted to create a toy car line that was a lot more exciting in nature with flashy spectra flame paint, California hot rod type designs, and one that would fly down the track. He wanted to create an exciting toy car line which was vastly different than any of the competitors' line up, which only consisted of replicas of modern-day production cars and trucks of the time.

The year was 1967 when the first Hot Wheels went into production. It would take another full year, when in 1968, the cars were released to the public for sale at retail outlets across America. They were an instant hit with young boys and girls and continue to this day, more than fifty-three years later. The "Original Sixteen" or "Sweet Sixteen" as some collectors refer to them, were the first models released by Mattel in 1968. They were the Beatnik Bandit, Custom Barracuda, Custom Camaro, Custom Corvette, Custom Cougar, Custom Eldorado, Custom Firebird, Custom Fleetside, Custom Mustang, Custom T-Bird, Custom Volkswagen, Deora, Ford J-Car, Hot Heap, Python, and Silhouette. The cars were something to behold, and never lost their grip on the toy car market to this day. The coolness and "fun factor" were through the roof, and only gained steam as time went on with innovative new designs, race sets, and accessories as they were produced by the incredible and creative minds at Mattel, Inc.

The Original 16 Hot Wheels Released in 1968

Mattel, along with their designers, engineers, and factory workers, created some of the most innovative and amazing accessories of the time that still make me shake my head in disbelief to this day. They were way ahead of their time in every respect. From the multiple and different race sets produced, to the Tune-Up Tower, Super Chargers, Rod Runner, Snake and Mongoose line-up of cars and sets; they had it all going on. It was not just the metal spectra flame cars, their accessories, and race sets that captured our imaginations either. Sizzlers appeared on the scene in 1970 and I think we all needed resuscitation once laying our eyes and hands on these ground-breaking creations. They were rechargeable, battery controlled 1:64 scale plastic cars that would rip around the "Fat Track" at what seemed like hundreds of miles per hour. Yes, I said, "Fat Track" and I am proud of it. The "Fat Track" was this huge, high banked, oval, black plastic track layout that was released coincidingly with the Sizzlers line. Wow, this was truly something to behold over fifty years ago. We just could not believe that accessories like the "Juice Machine" and "Power Pit" would recharge these little babies and they would literally rip around the track racing one another. It is a wonder we do not all have neck injuries for those of us who played with these cars back in 1970 and on. Our heads would literally move with our favorite car as it flew around the track as we cheered it on to victory. Pit Stops were needed, depending on the length and type of race that you and your friends decided on. It was truly a thing of beauty, and I really wish I could shake all the hands of the individuals who created this amazing toy line.

The Amazing Sizzlers and the Famous FAT TRACK

Mattel continued to produce the redline era cars until the mid to late seventies, at which time they were all transitioned to black wall tires. It was the end of the greatest era of Hot Wheels, of course, in my humble opinion.

Chapter 3

MY APPROACH

Over the last three decades of collecting, I always get asked the same questions; "How do you do it?" "Why do you do it?" "How come I can't find even one original Hot Wheels collection?" Well, it has never been a secret on how I search out and consistently dig up original, Redline Era one owner childhood Hot Wheels collections. In this chapter I will explain my passion for what I do and why. Later I will reveal, in detail, all the things that I have done in the past and what I do now that ultimately and consistently brings me dozens of collections, and thousands of Redline Era Hot Wheels cars, sets, and accessories year after year.

Some in the hobby call me the "Indiana Jones" of Hot Wheels, due to, what is considered, my incredible success in finding amazing original Redline Era Hot Wheels collections over the past three decades. For the record, I do not buy from long standing collectors, and I do have my reasons. The main reason is that there really is not much of a challenge doing it this way and I cannot verity the provenance, not only of the entire collection, but of every individual car and race set contained within it. It is vitally important to me, as a passionate collector, to be able to have the utmost confidence in what I am buying. I am always fascinated with all the interesting people I meet along the way and their individual stories regarding their collections. Fascinating to say the least.

I have always only searched out original Redline Era Hot Wheels collections that have been shoved away in attics, basements, storage units, garages, and people's closets. The excitement and extreme challenge of the hunt, and what I like to call the "capture", is what truly drives me to do what I do. The "hunt" is the searching aspect of what I do. The "capture" is closing the deal once I have the collection in my sights. It is a remarkably simple way of describing what I do, and I will take a much deeper and more detailed dive into the "How I do it" in a later chapter. My desire to become an Archaeologist as a child growing up still rages inside me. I genuinely believe that digging up original one owner Redline Era Hot Wheels collections is just one way to satisfy my lifelong desire of becoming an Archaeologist. I just love finding these collections in the "wild."

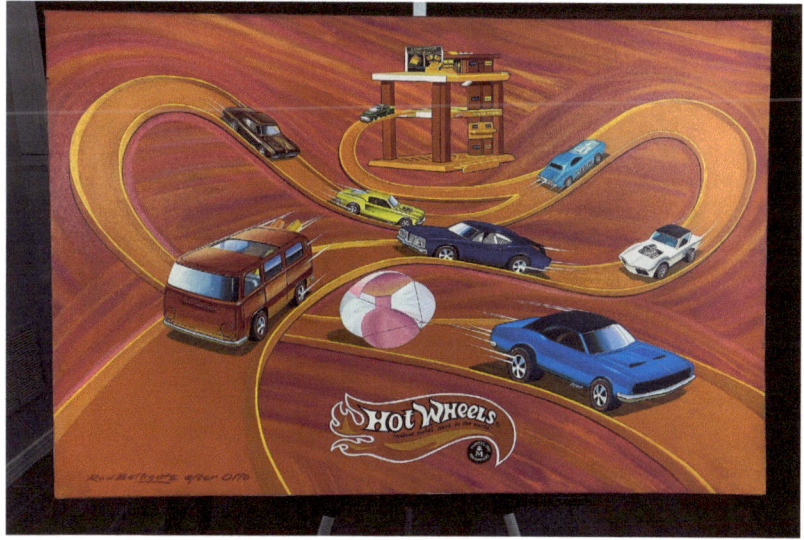

Painting in the spirit of Otto Kuhni done by Rodney Bathgate from Australia who is also a deeply passionate Redline Hot Wheels Collector.

I have to say, that even after all these 30 years of collecting original Redline Hot Wheels as an adult, it still gives me a total rush and feeling of sheer enjoyment after finding an original one owner Hot Wheels collection from the sixties or seventies. A feeling that has never diminished at any level with the passing of time or the amount of collections that I have discovered. The feeling is the same as it was when I unearthed my first original collection out of Woodbury, NJ in the Fall of 1992. The best way for me to describe it is like waking up on Christmas morning and knowing that there are amazing things just waiting for you under the tree. What utterly amazes me is that the amount of original Hot Wheels collections that are still out there in the "wild." For some reason, and for many years, collectors in the hobby think that the market has dried up for finding original collections at Flea Marts, Yard Sales, Garage Sales, etc., but I am living proof that the stuff is still out there and there is certainly still plenty of it just waiting to be brought to light. I am more than happy to take the task on and oblige those that want to sell their collections. Always consider, the number of cars that Mattel Inc. was churning out during the first five to ten years of production. Literally millions of these cars were produced and enjoyed by many children during that time and continue to this day. The thing that truly boggles my mind over the past 5 years, is the overall condition that some of the original collections that I discover are still found in. I find collections, even today, that look like they were either just pulled off the factory line or recently ripped out of their blister packs. Not sure how this is even possible as I and all my friends played with these cars and enjoyed them immensely for years. My childhood collection was in good shape when I was reunited with it in 1992, but I say with certainty that they all were far from factory or blister pack fresh. Considering that this toy car line was first produced in 1967 and released in 1968, some of these cars are now over fifty- four years old and counting. I wish I looked that good after fifty-four years.

Redline Hot Wheels being produced at the Mattel headquarters in Hawthorne, CA circa 1970

My quest continues and I do not see any end in sight. How could I possibly consider retiring from something that gives me such enjoyment and fulfillment? The hobby continues to occupy a lot of my time and I continue to absolutely enjoy every second of it. Not sure what the next year or five years of collecting will bring, but I am certain that there are a lot of the Redline Hot Wheels just waiting patiently for "Indy" to pay a visit.

Chapter 4

THE APPRAISAL

A big piece of the puzzle of securing and purchasing original Hot Wheels collections from the sixties and seventies when they show their beautiful little faces, is the appraisal process. Let me get this out of the way before we move on. NEVER SEND THE APPRAISAL IN WRITING. Period, end of story. Over the years, I have learned that a small percentage of sellers will "weaponize" it and use it against you to squeeze more money out of another buyer. It is just not fair, for me personally and as a passionate collector, that offers FREE appraisals, to have them used against me for selfish reasons. The strange thing is, almost every time that this has happened to me, the seller(s) inevitably has never come back for a counteroffer. It is a weird dynamic, but I have learned not to put any appraisals in writing. You have been properly warned.

First and foremost, you must engage with the seller or sellers, and a fair amount of the time you end up dealing with both a husband-and-wife team. Many times, you will also deal with sons or daughters and even grandchildren or nieces and nephews who have had the collections left to them following the passing of the original owner. You must earn their trust and respect within a very abbreviated span of time, whether on the phone or in person. The best advice I can give is to always be upfront and honest with people who reach out to you to sell their collections. Keep in mind the sentimental value that sometimes hangs onto these cars like a barnacle. A lot of people who end up either reaching out to me via email or on my cell phone always tell me that they have done their homework and research and know exactly what the values are of each car in their collection. The unfortunate part is that they almost never seem to take condition, color, or specific casting into account when valuing their cars. This is where you will have to put your teaching cap on, be very patient, and try to educate them on what determines value. For the most part, sellers always think that their collections are worth mint prices and sometimes way above full retail. Ebay has a funny way of convincing the public or sellers in this case, that every car is worth an exorbitant amount of money which is based on "Buy It Now" auctions. Keep this in mind when discussing values and why Ebay may not be the best place to gather the most recent value or pricing of Redline Era Hot Wheels if you do not know what you are looking for. Most of the time, sellers will understand the concept of only looking at recent completed auctions of the last thirty to sixty days of a comparable car instead of only looking at "Buy It Now" prices. If you explain this concept to them properly and calmly, most of the time they will get it. I literally must address this over ninety percent of the time with the owners of these rare collections. It is quite a common theme of the initial call or email I receive when I am engaged in the process.

Once you have established a good rapport with the sellers along with an open line of communication, it is now time to collect information and get the story, or what I like to call, the collection's provenance. Provenance is defined as: *the place of origin or earliest known history of something.* For me personally, this is vitally important to me as a collector to know the complete story as it relates to the collection. I have uncovered collections over the years that were either originally from a Mattel employee at the Hawthorne, CA site or had a connection to one. If I were not persistent in my methods and did not take the time to gather this information, certain cars in some of these collections would have gone not only unnoticed but considered a custom by a lot of collectors in the hobby. Having the provenance on a collection is vital to its authenticity and reflective of the overall value. I would never purchase a collection without gathering its provenance first.

Once all the information on the history or provenance of the collection is gathered, it is time to move onto the valuation of each individual car, carrying cases, button, sticker sheet, race set, and accessory. Take the time to thoroughly evaluate each car and item individually. It may overwhelm you at times with certain large collections, but in the end, it is the most responsible and accurate way of appraising a collection. Seeing, holding, and examining the cars and other items in person is ideal but not always possible or reasonable. I generally appraise and purchase collections from states and countries that would require a long plane ride to view the cars in person. For me, this just is not feasible, and I really do not have the time to commit to something like this. If a collection is not within a two- or three-hour drive of my home base, then it gets a little tricky. The size of the collection will determine how many total pictures you will need to review. I always ask for views of each car from the top, bottom, both sides, front, and back. I also stress to the seller(s) that the pictures need to be in high definition, in focus, and well lit. Most people understand and send great pictures to review. The positives are, however, the new smart phones have incredible high-density cameras that produce noticeably clear pictures. I offer options for the sellers to either email me the pictures to my Gmail account or text message pictures to me on my iPhone. It seems to work better for everyone to send pictures of the cars through text messaging. They are much more easily accessed and offer the same clarity and high definition that the computers do.

Moving on, let us explore the most important aspect of evaluating the entire collection, specifically each car individually. The cars are what we all chase and hold the most value. When I begin to evaluate a car, I always take a brief scan at the overall condition immediately and then move onto the four tires. Gathering the provenance plays a huge and particularly important role in this aspect of the appraisal as well. What I mean by this is that I rely on the history of the collection so that I can be confident in what I am looking at. Furthermore, the provenance establishes trust that I can be sure that the cars were not tampered with over the years. This is true ninety-nine percent of the time. This is one of the main reasons that, as a rule over the past three decades of collecting, I do not purchase collections from collectors. Collectors tend to swap out wheels and do other things to the cars to improve not only the look of an individual piece, but also increase its' value. There is nothing wrong with this, but I only want things that are original with patina, no matter how good or bad it may be. Originality is king to this Redline Archaeologist.

Chief Redline Archaeologist Bob Young Examining and Appraising a Hot Wheels Value

Getting down to the Nitty Gritty (Kitty). Come on, I just had to. The next step in the valuation of a car is to begin with the wheels. The best starting point are the four wheels. It really does tell a large portion of the cars play and storage history. The chrome, red line continuity, and overall look tell me a ton regarding how much or little the car was or was not played with way back when. Keep in mind that storing cars in the cases and in extreme environments can affect the cars paint and wheel chrome as well. Humidity, salt air along the coasts, heat, and cold can severely damage these precious little gems over time. Those dastardly Sizzlers can wreak havoc, not only on themselves, but on the cars that border them in the storage cases where they lie as well. The acid that leaks or leeches out of the Sizzlers from their rechargeable batteries over time can destroy a car's paint, chrome, and bases. I have witnessed it many times in my career and it always seems to be the most valuable cars in the collection that get affected the most severely. Well, it seems that way anyway.

Getting back to the wheels. When all four tires appear to look new with all the chrome shiny and a complete, undisturbed, and a noticeably clear red line completely encircling the outer part of it, you can be assured that the car was basically never run down the infamous orange track. The orange track tended to strip a cars wheel chrome and erase the red line with repeated play. The sides of the orange track have a small rim on both sides that the cars would rub against repeatedly while racing. It just was what it was, and the cars were made to be played with, and a lot. Now that you have established play wear as non-existent, minor, moderate, or major, it is now time to move on to the next step of evaluating the car's true value.

Un-played With
Vs
Played with Condition Wheels

The next step in the process is to look at the front and back portions of the car. I always utilize jeweler's headband type magnifying glasses when appraising a collection. You will see things that the naked eye just cannot pick up. The reason I look at the front and back areas is to further evaluate play wear, if any, and here are some things to look for. You will need to look for wear or chips on the front tips of the hood or fenders, especially when it comes to the customs. Most other castings of Redline era cars will also demonstrate play wear as well on the front ends. Chips or scratches in the flat black painted grills of cars like the Classic '31 Ford Woody or the Classic '32 Ford Vicky may also be visible. The rear ends of the cars will show nicks, chips, and scratches as well if the cars were run down the track or played with. The reason for this type of wear to these cars is that sometimes cars would slam into the back of another car or wall during play. It was quite common for us youngsters of the sixties and seventies to run multiple cars down a racetrack without taking cars that were previously run off the track to clear a path. It is just how it was when we enjoyed these cars and race sets. So, as you can see, this factors, not only into the amount of play that a car exhibits, but also affects its' overall value.

Front worn grill of a Classic '32 Ford Vicky Vs untouched front grill of a Hot Heap

Now we move onto the overall quality of paint on the car. There are many things that can go wrong with a toy car's paint, especially a car that is not only over fifty years old, but one that has endured extremes of temperature and humidity in storage over time. There are many factors that influence the quality of a car's paint. Lots of problems related to a car's paint are the result of the amount and type of play wear that a car endures over time, and they are, chips, scratches, and nicks. These all affect the car's value negatively and depending on how rough the car was played with will be a big factor in lessening a car's value. Paint toning is another term that seasoned collectors in the hobby throw around quite often. Paint toning is the "darkening" of spots on the car or the entire car's paint. Sometimes the hood is toned where the rest of the body appears untoned. This was due to the hood being painted at a different time or location within Mattel's factory. Hong Kong versus US produced cars do show distinct differences in paint toning.   Other descriptions defined are what we call in the hobby "spot toning" or "wispy toning." Spot toning is where small spots in all different shapes and sizes occur and darken only those areas. Wispy toning can be described as though a light paint brush passed over the car in spots and caused a slightly darker and a swirly look to the paint. Toning dramatically drops the value of a car and appears often on some of the 1968 and 1969 customs like the Eldorado, Charger, AMX, and Mustang to name a few.

Examples of paint toning on a Green Custom Cougar and Orange Classic '57 Bird

Finally, the last step is to examine the base and all the plastic pieces including the windshields, domes, and canopies reflective of each casting. The base is important to a significant number of collectors and can make or break a car's individual value to some collectors. I am not one of those that place a huge value on the quality or shininess of a car's base. In all my years of hunting down these cars and collections, and visiting with many fellow collectors, I can honestly say that I have never seen a car displayed upside down. Obviously, I am just making a point that the base does not affect a car's overall value to me unless it is totally tarnished or what we call in the hobby, a "crumbler." There are two castings that I have come across over the years that I have identified as "crumblers" and they were the 1971 Bye Focal and 1971 Iced T. The base of the 1971 Bye Focal and 1971 Iced T are thought to have had a poor-quality metal poured during production which has caused this defect to occur. Always inspect a Bye Focal or Iced T's base prior to purchasing it, even if it is still in its original blister pack. One with a "crumbler" base basically has zero value or is a parts car.

Missing parts also play a significant role in determining value. Lots of examples of cars that pop up in original collections with missing parts are the Beatnik Bandit (engine), Silhouette (engine), Hot Heap (engine),

Python (engine), Chapparral 2G (wing), Swingin' Wing (wing), OLDS 442 (spoiler), Deora (surf boards), Volkswagen Beach Bomb (surf boards), Classic Cord (roof), Grass Hopper (roof), Power Pad (camper), Sky Show Fleetside (ramp), Sky Show Deora (ramp), Mighty Maverick (wing), Seasider (boat), Fuel Tanker (hoses), Iced T (roof), Jet Threat (driver's canopy), Mutt Mobile (roof, back gate, dogs), S'Cool Bus (engine blower), Short Order (back trunk), T-4-2 (roof), and Funny Money (bumper). Sometimes, depending on the overall condition of the car itself, the parts may hold a higher value than the car itself.

Cracked, broken, and scratched windshields, canopies, or domes on these cars also places a negative impact on a car's overall value. Lots of Hot Wheels were left on the family room floors by us kids, and parents or siblings would inevitably step on them. Well, I think you can see where I am going with this. Typically, the car's front and or back windshields, canopies, or domes always took the brunt of a family member's foot. This too affects a car's value significantly in the wrong direction. The amazing Rod Runner or Dual Rod Runner track accessory tended to scratch a car's dome or roof as well, dependent upon the number of times an individual car ran through either one or both.

The end result of a family member's foot on this beautiful purple Maserati Mistral. Notice the cracked front and back windshields.

Now that you have evaluated every aspect of the individual car, it is time to come up with a number on its value. Experience from doing this hundreds of times over the past thirty years has certainly taught me a lot about assessing a car's value. Well, let's hope anyway. I am a noticeably confident collector when it comes to understanding each of these unique and individual car's values, but fortunately or unfortunately, depending on how you look at it, the market does tend to change on a dime and significantly at times. When the market changes, I also need to change the value I place on a car or collection following a complete and thorough evaluation. Another aspect that takes time following a collections appraisal is to educate the seller(s) on their cars. Most of the time it is unexpected yet greatly appreciated when all is said and done. Once my appraisal is completed, I always schedule a time to talk on the phone with the seller(s) to discuss many things as it relates to their collection. In my humble opinion, I think it is critically important that they get all the facts, and usually by the end of the call, they cannot thank you enough.

Educating the sellers takes time but has been the one thing that has landed me more collections over the years than any other aspect of the appraisal process. People genuinely appreciate the facts explained to them especially when coming into this process not knowing much other than what they find on Ebay or other internet sites, including social media. There is a ton of information out there related to the original first ten years of production of the Redline era Hot Wheels. Some good and some not so good for the hobby. I cannot stress enough the importance of being upfront and honest with the seller(s). It goes a long way with purchasing these incredible collections and can make or break a deal. I am living proof that this works and is an incredibly important part of the appraisal process.

Let us get to the education part of the appraisal. First, I bring them the good news and go over the cars within the collection that, in my opinion, have the most value. Keep in mind that they may not be the rarest or most desirable. Everything in my world as a passionate Redline Hot Wheels collector is all about condition. As in the words of Jan Brady, "Condition, Condition, Condition". Overall condition of a car determines the value of a car, not necessarily its rarity. You may have a magenta OLDS 442 that is missing its spoiler and stickers and has been played with to the point of missing a significant amount of its original paint. To me, the value of the rarest and most desirable production car just bottomed out. Some may disagree, but I would take a blister pack fresh magenta Short Order any day of the week over a beat up OLDS 442. Sorry to disappoint, but the quality of a car determines the greatest value to this Redline collector.

Sometimes I get original collections in that have over ninety percent of the cars contained within it in blister pack condition or like they were just pulled off the factory line at Mattel, Inc. When this happens, you need to be patient and discuss all the cars that have value typically over one hundred dollars each. Sellers love to hear that their collection has been well cared for, and because of that, has much greater value across the board. Obviously, passing on the right and truthful information will cost you more, but chances are you will be the only one doing it.

Beaters with little to no value vs blister pack fresh cars with a lot of value based on overall condition

Secondly, I deliver the bad news. It always seems to be a better approach and continues to work well for me to this day to give the good news initially. I discuss things like why a car that could have had a lot of value actually does not, which is typically due to play wear and or the storage environment. I also talk about cars that are missing parts and the decrease in value due to this fact. Sometimes the parts are worth more than the car itself depending on casting and condition. I then venture into all the common castings in the most common colors and talk about why their values are what they are. At this point, I am just about done with the entire appraisal and it is usually when I present the collection's full retail value and my very generous offer.

Chapter 5

THE OFFER

In my opinion, the offer is the most challenging part of securing a collection and bringing the cars home. My reasons are multiple, so let us get started. Developing an open line of communication, being fair, and honest are the three most important aspects of landing the deal. You must first and foremost develop an open line of communication with the owner of the collection. Whatever your preference of communication, you must respond quickly and thoroughly when a lead comes in on a collection. The only thing to assume is that on the other end of the phone or email is the most incredible one owner Hot Wheels collection ever, just waiting to come home to roost. Go into every conversation optimistically and with a positive attitude. I hear it all the time from sellers that other collectors that they contacted were overly aggressive and somewhat hostile during their initial conversation. This has never made any sense to me, especially with the nature of this hobby. If you are truly a passionate Hot Wheels collector, then you should have a smile on your face like the Cheshire Cat from Alice in Wonderland when discussing your favorite toy car line. The best advice I can give with your approach to communicating with an owner of an amazing collection is to be kind, patient, and let them tell the story. The initial conversation has always been one of the best moments for me in the entire process. Remember, you only get one opportunity to make a good first impression.

Secondly, you must be fair, period, exclamation point! If you go into this trying to maximize your profit on every single car in a collection, you will fail miserably almost every time. You may get lucky with an unsuspecting owner or someone that did not take the time to do their due diligence on what approximate value their collection holds, but most of the time you will fail in making the purchase. Paying a fair price is not only good for the seller, but is also good for us, the collector and buyer. When both parties are happy, then the deal is a good one. This approach has never failed me in thirty years of searching for the original Redline Hot Wheels. People will appreciate you for not only taking the time to educate them on their collection, but also for making a fair and more than reasonable offer.

Third and finally, be honest with the seller(s). Honesty can be tough for some people, but without it, individuals will throw up red flags all during the negotiations and the deal is usually dead at that point. I have seen it happen to other collectors over the years, and some just never get it. Generally, sellers are not stupid and can sense someone's dishonest behavior, especially if they have done their homework or have received my appraisal with all the information that goes with it. I cannot tell you how many times sellers have circled back to me after shopping their collection around to other buyers following my appraisal. Ninety-nine times out of a hundred, I usually end up with the collection. I am not boasting, I am just stating facts that my approach and methods have been proven hundreds if not thousands of times over in my career. I have always shared a lot of these experiences and stories with my small circle of reputable collectors on how some other collectors and buyers are responsible for my success at some level due to their approach and behavior. For some reason, sellers always like to share their horror stories with me of shopping their collections around to other potential buyers and collectors. From buyers getting angry with the seller(s) when the deal goes south because of the buyer's aggressive behavior and extremely low ball offers, to all the misinformation that they try to pass on to them as the truth, thus trying to steal the collection out from under them. They always thank me emphatically for taking the time, educating them, and making a more than fair and generous offer. I also offer to split or pay all the shipping costs in some cases when I get the sense that every dollar counts to the seller. Sometimes, I even receive a referral from them. I typically end up with another collection from an incredibly happy seller who spreads the word to friends and relatives that have their old Redline Era Hot Wheels still in storage.

Now the issue of what percentage of total appraised retail value do you pay so that the offer is considered fair and reasonable. The percentage that has been most successful for me over the years has been around fifty to eighty percent of full retail value based on the final appraisal and size and quality of the collection. I have always explained my justification for offering less than full retail, and normally sellers agree with the rationale. I always explain that I can typically find any car I desire and pay full retail anywhere on the internet, including EBay and all the Facebook auction sites. I also have carrying costs to what I do to continually dig up these original one owner Redline Era Hot Wheels collections, and we will take a much more thorough and deeper dive into this later.

Chapter 6

FINALIZING THE DEAL

Now comes the next most challenging part of the deal, and that is agreeing on the "exchange." This is where it can get a little tricky to say the least. By the word "exchange" I mean swapping the collection for the agreed upon funds. In other words, getting the cars and handing over the cash. In my three decades of hunting down and capturing one owner Redline Hot Wheels collections, all my deals have gone smoothly, except for one back in 2016. I was robbed through Western Union of nine hundred dollars by an individual who chose not to send me the final half of a collection after I sent full payment. Twenty-Five years of trusting people in this hobby was destroyed in one fell swoop. I am a very trusting person who always sees the good in people. Everyone has my respect until they do not, but that is on them. Way back in the nineties and early two thousands, all my deals were local to where I called home in the southern New Jersey region, right outside of Philadelphia. I would always go to the sellers' home with a friend or meet them at a designated, agreed upon, neutral and public location. My collector friend Todd Deschaine usually accompanied me on many of my early discoveries. Some neighborhoods that Todd and I ventured into over the years were not exactly Shangri la. It was the right and smart thing to do to bring a companion along, especially one that is six foot four and a bit intimidating. It always worked out well and I never ran into any issues, except for the occasional cigarette smoke filled home or angry growling dog or two. Cash was always king, but I did get the occasional individual who preferred a money order or certified bank check. I never understood this and probably never will, but I always obliged.

So, the big question remains; "How do you safely make payment and receive the collection from great distances so that both parties are comfortable with the exchange?" Currently, there are a lot of internet trolls and dishonest individuals who are in the business of ripping people off, so we must be on guard and cognizant of this at all times. I hope I do not come off as sounding paranoid, but this is a stark reality to the times we currently live in. Dealing with this aspect of the deal after the price has been agreed upon by both parties remains one of the most difficult aspects, and for many reasons. First, they do not know me, and I certainly do not know them. These days, with many of my amazing finds, contact initially is made via email, from my "Contact Page" on my website, www.RedlineArcheology.com. We are complete strangers from the outset. Therefore, you must gain trust immediately and open a line of communication as previously discussed. If not, the deal will vanish almost instantly following the first conversation. I have learned from my mistakes over the years and choose not to repeat them.

The appraisal is complete, negotiations are over, and now the difficult discussion of how it works on my end must be addressed with the seller(s). The first questions inevitably from the seller(s) at this juncture is "How does it work with shipping the cars and getting paid?" or "What are the next steps?" I very clearly explain that I do not and will not send any form of payment before receiving the collection on my end first and foremost. I am always clear and concise with my instructions on packing and shipping the cars, cases, accessories, and race sets safely and efficiently. Sellers do follow directions almost all the time. I say almost all the time because I inevitably end up getting one out of a hundred that just did not listen, and the cars are typically scattered loose throughout the package or box upon arrival. It happens rarely but be prepared for when it does. It never is a pleasant experience, and it kind of ruins your day a bit. Just to be clear that If this is the worst thing that happens to you in a day, you are still way ahead in the game of life.

A collection of original Redline Era Hot Wheels

I further explain that I offer any form of reasonable payment methods that they are comfortable with once I receive the agreed upon collection. The higher percentage of the time, most sellers are fine with me sending a personal check that displays my name and home address. I usually will send it United States Postal Service Flat Rate Priority Mail so the check can be tracked by the seller(s). I will also text message a picture of the check, tracking number, and shipping box prior to dropping it in the mail. This is my preferred method of making payment as well because I do have a safety net if things go south. I can always cancel the check if I do not receive the collection as agreed upon in a reasonable amount of time. For the record, I have never had to cancel any payment over thirty years of hunting down the Redline Hot Wheels. PayPal, Venmo, Money Orders, and Certified Bank Checks all run a distant second regarding forms of payment that sellers choose. I always agree to any of these methods of payment if I receive the cars first. I have only had to walk away from a couple of collections over the years due to the uncomfortableness on either mine, the seller(s), or on both parties' ends.

Both parties have agreed to the terms of packing, shipping method, and type of payment. Next step is to swap pictures of the shipping box(es), USPS tracking numbers, and payment method. I always text message pictures from my end with the payment details and request text message pictures on their end. It is the quickest, most accessible, easiest, and most understandable way of doing it. Sellers always seem comfortable with exchanging the information this way and it typically puts both of our minds at ease. It works every time and I strongly recommend this method of exchange. This is how I have learned over the years through trial and error and the changing times, to streamline an exceedingly difficult thing into a very trusting experience for all involved.

Chapter 7

The "How To" Guide to Finding Original Hot Wheels Collections

Let me start off by making a particularly important blanket statement. To be successful in finding and scoring these rare Redline Era Hot Wheels collections, you must approach this like you would any start up business. There, I got that off my chest, so here we go. Pay close attention as I am going to take a very deep dive on how I do what I do, and why. You will not find this information anywhere in the hobby, so prepare to take notes.

I guess I could make the argument that I have been a deeply passionate Redline Hot Wheels collector since 1968 which would put me at fifty-three years now, but I just cannot make this claim. Hot Wheels, for me as a child of the sixties, were only a toy that was meant to be played with and enjoyed. I say it over and over that I never thought in a million years that these little toy cars that were under a dollar each in the stores back in the day, would ever be worth more than that, a single dollar. Well, you know my story by now, so I can certainly say with the utmost confidence that I have been and continue to be an extremely passionate collector of the Redline Hot Wheels going on thirty years now. It was, and always will be, my most favorite childhood toy, and one that produced some of the greatest and fun memories from my earliest childhood years.

My adult journey as a collector began in the Fall of 1992. I began my quest for searching and hunting down original, one owner childhood Redline era Hot Wheels collections after finding out from my mother that these little toy cars might have value. Mattel was poised to celebrate their twenty-fifth anniversary of their most popular and greatest boy's toy line in 1993 which was just over the horizon. News stories started to surface in the media in 1992 regarding Mattel's upcoming twenty-fifth anniversary celebration and I began to scratch my head thinking that my childhood collection of seventy-two cars, sets, and accessories may be worth something more than a dollar a piece.

I was born to be an entrepreneur, and the business part of my brain started to engage. I started thinking about how I could first, sell my collection for top dollar and second, how I could find more of these original Redline Era Hot Wheels collections to sell. My wife and I were just starting out and did not have a lot of money and this might be a way to help pay some bills, especially my college loans. I knew all my childhood friends owned lots of Hot Wheels growing up and they would end up being my first targeted market to go after. I struck out locating most of them, and the friends I did contact had no idea where their old Hot Wheels were or knew that their parents either gave them away to a relative or friend or threw them out when they went off to college. I was not only bummed out with these answers but totally shocked that their parents would ditch their prized Hot Wheels collections. At this point, I was out of options and had to put my entrepreneurial thinking cap on and get to work.

Times were different in 1992. We did not have hundreds of cable channels at our fingertips, Netflix was still five years away from its beginnings, and we had the newspaper delivered to our front doorsteps every day, and even on Sunday mornings. The Sunday paper was always the most anticipated edition of the week. Not only was it the most extensive coverage in each section, but it had a lot of valuable coupons that everyone would clip. Lots of people would buy the Sunday edition just for the coupon section. The reason I bring this up is that there was also the Classified Ad section that I always loved to peruse through each week. I would always go right to the automotive section looking for deals on used cars, especially the exotics, that I certainly could not afford at the time, but I was and still am a dreamer of sorts.

One Sunday I guess I was bored in a sense, so I decided to read the other sections of the classifieds when I stumbled upon a sub-section that was titled "Wanted to Buy." I decided to see what this "Wanted to Buy" sub-section was all about, so I ventured forward. It ended up being the answer to my dilemma on how I would go about searching out these Hot Wheels that I knew were still hiding in basements, attics, garages, and people's homes all throughout southern New Jersey and southeastern Pennsylvania areas. This "Wanted to Buy" section had everything from subscribers that were looking for old furniture, appliances, Barbie dolls, slot cars, and any old toys in general. It was the perfect platform for getting the word out to tens of thousands of readers each week. I immediately picked up the phone, you know, the one that hung on the wall with the long retractable ugly green or yellow cord that you had to dial. Ok, ok, it was push button, but I just could not resist. I do remember the phone that my grandparents had when I was real young. They had a working phone that had a black ear cup attached to a black cord that you had to hold up to your ear at the same time you had to speak into this cup shaped thing on the phone telling the operator the number you wanted to call. Yes, the rumors are true, I am an old fart. I could never reach it anyway and was always told not to touch it or go near it. We always listened to our parents and grandparents back then, because if you did not, well, let's just say that it did not ever end well. I never knew what happened to that piece of telecommunication history, but I can guess that it probably ended up at a yard sale or in the trash.

The original Courier-Post building located in Merchantville, NJ where the first classified ad was created

I immediately called the Courier-Post and asked for the Classified Ad department. I was put in touch with a rather gruff, unenthused sounding representative. Undeterred, I proceeded to ask all the questions pertaining to placing a classified ad, specifically one in the "Wanted to Buy" section. Following what sounded like a puff on a cigarette, she began to explain all the details and the associated cost for running an ad for a day versus a week versus a month. I almost fell off my chair when I heard just how much this venture was going to set me back. One hundred and eleven dollars a week for a three-line ad in the "Wanted to Buy" section. I was literally and figuratively speechless. This was outrageous in my mind, but I had to compose myself, walk to the edge of the cliff and take the leap, hoping to hit warm Caribbeanesque water. My funds were extremely limited back then, but my entrepreneurial risk-taking spirit kicked in and I ordered a three-line seven-day ad that began that day, on Sunday. It was not until the final day that the ad ran on the following Saturday that I finally hit spectraflame gold. It was a small twenty-four car orange flat case made by Mattel chock full of Redline Hot Wheels. I was so excited and continued to run the ad until it finally fizzled out weeks later. I just could not afford to run the ad over long periods of time due to our limited finances. We did not have the expendable income that would allow or support running this ad week after week. Over the next 10 years, through my experience with running this three-line classified ad in the "Wanted to Buy" section of the Courier-Post and eventually the Philadelphia Inquirer newspapers, I learned that the month of May was ideal for finding collections. This was mostly due to people in the area cleaning out their garages, attics, and basements during Springtime. It is a big part of the culture in the northeastern part of this country and something I was all too familiar with.

The Grass Roots Approach

What I do is unearth original, childhood Redline Era Hot Wheels collections that have been hiding away for decades. How I do it has never been a secret in the hobby as far as I am concerned. This is the part that has always bewildered myself and my friends that even to this day, I have not created a bunch of people or competitors that try to imitate my exceedingly successful approach. I also try to help other collectors find local collections in their respective areas so they can enjoy the feeling that I get on a fairly frequent basis. To this day, I really think it is important for the hobby to share the excitement and all the rare cars and collections that I discover from all over this country and abroad with other passionate Redline collectors. Let us get started on what I call the "Grass Roots Approach" to finding the original childhood Redline Era Hot Wheels collections.

I began my collecting career as an adult and on a very tight budget. I still believe that you can find these collections on an extremely limited budget even to this day if you use the right multi-pronged approach like I did early on. There are many ways to "skin a cat" or "score a collection" in this hobby. I have seen what works and what falls flat. When I first started attempting to score collections in the nineties, my methods matured and became more diverse over time. I went from only running a simple three-line classified ad a few times a year to implementing a few things to hopefully bring even more amazing collections home. Some of the other weapons in my arsenal to uncover original collections were Business Cards and paper Flyers.

The Business Card

The business card was the first thing that I had produced following the initial success of my classified ad in the Courier-Post newspaper. I made it as simple of a design as possible, with still getting my point across in a truly clear and discernable way. The simpler the design, the less money I had to put out of my pocket was the underlying reason. To this day, I have never been afraid to take risks and spend money on marketing, but at that time, it just was not available to me. The final design of my first business card read:

I BUY OLD TOYS
Hot Wheels * Johnny Lightnings

Top Dollar Paid	Call Anytime
$$$$$$$$$$$$$$	Phone Number

Choices of graphics were very elementary and few and far between at the time. This was the early nineties and computerized graphic art was in its' early years of development. I could not find any graphics that resembled a recognizable Hot Wheel car from the late sixties. I finally found a graphic that was the front end of a Corvette pointed straight at you. I placed it above the text as this was the obvious choice of placement on the card in my mind. The card was very reflective of my successful classified ad as far as the verbiage was concerned. The cost at the time was minimal from the local business supply store, especially the way I designed it and what paper stock I ordered, along with a one-color card. If I remember correctly, I spent just under ten dollars for five hundred cards. I had to keep costs down anywhere I could so that when It came time to run the classified ad, I would have the funds to support it. As soon as I got the call that the cards were ready for pick up, I raced to the store, paid for them, and got to work. Needless to say, I was ordering more cards by the end of the first month.

The original business card designed to bring in collections

I would never leave the house without stuffing about ten to twenty of the cards in my front pocket so that I would never miss an opportunity to pass them out. There were local toy shows, train shows, flea markets, garage sales, and yard sales that I felt would produce some of the lowest hanging fruit per se. In all these years, I have only run into one other collector in this hobby that had a business card on them that was similar in design to mine created to find vintage Hot Wheels. I like to think that they got the idea from me, but who knows. Every individual that I engaged at all the events would absolutely receive a business card from me personally or they would find one either on their table or under their windshield wiper on their car in the respective parking lot. I try to never leave any stone unturned. Never let an opportunity pass you by that may stir up a collection. You just never know who you are talking to. The restroom stalls were not immune to my business card either.

It is not only the toy shows and yard sales where you need to get the word out. Getting the word out to your friends, relatives, and neighbors is a great place to continue your quest of unearthing collections. I continually try to work my passion for collecting the Redline Era Hot Wheels into almost every conversation I have with people that surround me. Parties, bar-b-ques, and any type of social gathering, no matter how big or small, is an opportunity to let people know that you have a passion for the old Hot Wheels.

Whenever you walk into an antiques store, estate sale, garage sale, yard sale, or visit a flea market, always ask the owner, seller, or employee if they have any old Hot Wheels or Matchbox. For some reason, and it continues to this day, it seems like everyone thinks Hot Wheels are Matchbox cars. Matchbox obviously did a great job of branding from the earliest days of the 1950's. Therefore, you should always mention Matchbox when asking for Hot Wheels. Let them all know that you are a very generous buyer of the cars, cases, race sets, accessories, and entire collections as well. Never leave that part out of any conversation regarding these little gems or the fact that you offer free appraisals and pay a "Finders Fee." Finders fees are a good motivating factor to spur on people to start looking for the old Hot Wheels for you as well. I typically pay ten percent of the total cost paid for a collection to the individual who referred the collection to me. I have found some incredibly nice cars and collections over the years using this simple approach. Lots of these antique stores, and the dealers at flea markets, sometimes have cases full of cars either in the back of the store packed away or in the back of their cars behind their respective tables. Drop your business card in their hand as a common practice before you leave. You may be the first call they make if a nice collection comes into their possession in the future.

The workplace is another fantastic place to find collections as well. I have scored multiple collections over the years from co-workers and their relatives and friends. Understanding that the individuals that were born between the years of 1956 to 1966 have the greatest chance of possessing the cars from the first ten years of production at Mattel, Inc. Look for co-workers that appear to be your age or from the era of the first ten years of production, 1967-1977. The main take-away from this is to always try to capitalize on the situation at hand, no matter where you are. With practice, you will become very skillful at working your passion of collecting the original Redline Hot Wheels into almost every encounter and conversation. Final words of advice regarding the business cards….. Never leave home without them!

Flyers

Yes, I am a huge hockey fan and lifetime Philadelphia Flyers' fan as well. Sorry, all you Boston Bruins and New York Rangers' fans, but I do bleed orange and black. These, however, are not the "Flyers" I need to discuss; it is the flyers that you have probably seen over the years placed around town on telephone and traffic light poles. Ones that say, "I Buy Houses" or "Cleaning Services Available". You certainly get my drift. I am not recommending placing a flyer on a telephone or traffic light pole because you must always be aware of local and municipal codes and laws that may prohibit this sort of thing. Sometimes permits are required to post advertising on public or government property.

Early on in my search for original Hot Wheels, it was not an issue in my local area to do this type of advertising. Times have certainly changed, so please do your homework first before implementing this type of marketing strategy. What happened next is why I created a flyer to further increase my visibility locally as a vintage Hot Wheels collector and buyer. I wanted everyone to know that I was the guy who paid the most for these beauties. The lightbulb went on one day when I was checking out at the local grocery store. On my way out I just happened to look up to my right before I exited through the automatic doors and there it was, a community cork board that measured at least six feet by four feet. Business cards and flyers, yes flyers were strewn all about leaving extraordinarily little cork in view. It was a mess, but it was a fantastic and no cost opportunity to get my amazing flyer placed on it in a very strategic spot. The store's bulletin board was visibly a lot larger in size than the standard ones that you found above the wall-hanging phones in the kitchens back then. I had never seen a corkboard this big in my entire life. To this entrepreneur, it was brilliant. As time went on, it was apparent to me that these community bulletin boards were everywhere in other grocery stores and businesses of all shapes and sizes. They were also in break rooms at places of work in all types of venues. I found one in the high schools' faculty lounge where I was working at the time. Of course, I placed one there and I realized that every school in the district just had to have one as well. Guess what I proceeded to do? You guessed right. I drove around to each school in the district, including the maintenance building and superintendent's office, and slapped one of my flyers strategically in plain view and at eye level, on every available corkboard. In the sales and business world this is called "beating the path", and boy did I blaze a new trail. I was even cognizant on the placement of each flyer and invariably would move other flyers and business cards out of the way that, in my mind, were occupying the most valuable real estate on the respective board. Afterall, these were the Redline Hot Wheels, and we all know they, not only take precedence in every situation, but are always the coolest and most important thing out there, right? Everything else needs to take a backseat to our beloved Redlines.

Every home in the nineties had a small cork board where moms would typically hang notes for the family, an annual complimentary calendar from the local realty office, and the kids' accomplishments in school, sports, and their other activities. It was quite a common practice for every household to centralize announcements and family events above or next to the main phone in the kitchen on a standard two by three-foot bulletin board. The kids would always participate with hanging their tests from school and projects on the corkboards that received good grades as well. Their ribbons and medals would be on display for all to see and gawk over. Especially the relatives who would always make such a fuss in front of the kids. It was sort of a competitive sibling thing that proudly displayed each of their scholarly and athletic accomplishments. Cell phones, well, over time, unfortunately ended this practice in the typical American home. Bulletin boards are rarely found in homes these days, and it is just another memory of growing up that has virtually vanished from our culture and lives.

My creative senses started to flow, and I got right to work on my flyer that I kept telling myself was, not only going to be the greatest flyer ever seen by mankind, but it was going to bring me an avalanche of Redline Hot Wheels. What I call a "Redline-Alanche." As I was putting the flyer together, I remember that all I could think about, from that moment on, was a potential lost set of eyes that had a Hot Wheels collection from the sixties or seventies or know someone that did. I really needed to finish the flyer and fast. It was maddening to say the least, but this is how an entrepreneur thinks. I am quite sure that plenty of business owners out there can relate. The clock was ticking so I got right to work. I engaged the marketing aspect of my brain and started to think how this amazing piece of paper should look.

I approached the flyer in a few ways. It had to be colorful, get the point across immediately and completely, and had to be recognizable to those that had these collections. Colors were easy as the Mattel Hot Wheels logo and the spectraflame paint schemes took care of this aspect. Making it recognizable meant that I had to choose cars that were, in my mind, the most readily recognizable and identifiable as Hot Wheels to kids and parents of the sixties and seventies. There were a handful of cars that I felt were the best choices for this and they were the Paddy Wagon, Beach Bomb, Twinmill, Beatnik Bandit, Silhouette, Custom Camaro, and Deora. Over the years, reflecting on my choices of recognizable Hot Wheels, I realized that I had hit the bullseye early on in my marketing flyer.

A Replica of the First Flyer produced that was pinned on every local grocery store and businesses community bulletin boards.

I narrowed my choices down to three cars as I did not want to make the flyer too busy or haphazard. In the wonderful and exciting world of marketing, keeping it simple is the best and most effective approach. The Beachbomb took center stage and was flanked by the Twinmill and Beatnik Bandit. I added a couple of Hot Wheels' logos in the top corners to further catch the attention of passers-by. The language on the flyer was almost identical to my classified ad in the local newspaper. It was the best layout and approach to quickly get the point across within a few seconds. Sometimes this is all the time you have to effectively capture a lead. My business card was always tacked along the bottom of the flyer as well. Normally I would place five cards perpendicular to the flyer so that individuals could pull them off quite easily and take one. I got on my horse and went to work scouring the entire county for every business, public place, and government building I could find that offered a community or company bulletin board. I even found bulletin boards at our local park. It was located outside the public restrooms above the water fountains. I was literally finding them in places I never thought of. My strategy was to scour the area and place as many of the flyers and business cards as possible. What I did not initially realize was that my flyers and business cards needed to be replenished on a regular basis. I determined that, in my spare time and travels, I would try to check on my flyers in each location at least once a week.

Another strategy I put into motion with the flyers and business cards was to drive around older housing developments in the suburbs and leave both the flyer and my business card in or on the outside of mailboxes.

Nowadays you must be aware of the "No Solicitation" rules and laws that apply in certain neighborhoods and Home-Owners Associations. It is not as easy as it used to be but still worth a try. I calculated that if my return of investment and my marketing efforts only produced a one percent return, my phone would be ringing off the hook soon enough. I literally placed hundreds of my flyers and business cards all over homes in the southern New Jersey area. The main reason I would look for the older homes and developments was that these were remarkably similar in appearance to where I grew up. My instincts told me that this was my best shot of finding a collection in someone's attic or basement, and I was right again. The older neighborhoods and housing developments produced the greatest amount of collections and still do to this day. The custom flyers along with my business cards were two of my most effective marketing tools early on in my search for the original Redline Hot Wheels collections. I scored collection after collection as time went on, and a significant portion were generated from my canvassing of neighborhoods, stores, businesses, parks, schools, and everywhere an opportunity presented itself. I believed in what I was doing and was relentless in my pursuit. It continues to pay off even to this day.

The No Cost Publication

Finding ways to save money on a limited budget was something that I was always looking for. I discovered that there were many low-cost or FREE publications available to the public. A couple examples that were available and at my disposal were the Shoppers Guide and the Penny Saver. Both were small monthly local publications that were free to the public at a lot of convenience stores like 7-11 and Mini-Mart. Some were even home delivered at no cost to the customer. I soon realized that I could expand my reach to tens of thousands of more households with small ads placed in both publications. The cost at the time was about twenty-five percent of what I was paying in the larger newspapers I was utilizing. It was invariably a huge savings and one that I had to at least give a try for a few months. I added these two local publications to my marketing plan, and they did produce a few collections over time. Certainly not at the rate of the larger newspapers, but keep in mind their total circulation was one-tenth of the larger publications. The return of investment was in line with what the classified ads were bringing in retrospect.

Other local publications like community, swim club, apartment, and condo newsletters also presented themselves as viable platforms and options at zero cost. I just needed to identify friends and relatives that either were part of the respective communities where these monthly or quarterly publications were available or residents of the apartment and condo associations. Most of the time I either knew someone or someone that knew someone that could get my small ad placed in their monthly or quarterly papers. I had to go around the side and in the back door to get this accomplished, but it worked. Nowadays, these type of newsletter publications go out not only in printable format, but more frequently sent out in email blasts. The phone began to ring in response to these community newsletters and collections started to roll in. I always would track each phone call or "lead" as they came in so that I had some data on where I was getting the most bang for my FREE buck. My research told me that the fifty-five and older communities produced the most amount of collections. Once again, justifying what my entrepreneurial and business sense was constantly telling me to do. I continue, to this day, to take advantage of these opportunities when they arise.

The Local News, TV Shows, & Newspapers

I must give all the credit to my wonderful, beautiful, and most supportive wife Deborah for this angle and approach to marketing. Tapping into the local news outlets and cable TV shows was one that caught me off guard a little but made total sense to me once I wrapped my mind around it. It was brilliant. My wife took the liberty of reaching out to local news stations, cable TV shows, networks, and newspapers with a simple email explaining my background and the uniqueness of what I was doing in my search for the old Hot Wheels. This was around the time of the twenty-fifth and thirtieth anniversary celebrations of the toy car line by Mattel. I was amazed at how often I ended up either in the local newspapers and on the TV as part of a human-interest story. When I was featured on the local news stations, my segment was typically placed after the weather forecast at the end of the broadcast. I did not care when or how, just as long as I was getting myself and what I did out there on these news outlets that literally reached millions of people over time.

Bob "Indiana Jones" Young featured on CBS 8 News in San Diego, CA

This only cost me a little slice of my time, so it was never a big commitment that took time from my growing family. I would always clear my schedule to accommodate the last-minute decisions by the respective news outlet that wanted to do a story on me, even if I had to take a personal day off from work. This is the nature of the news business especially when doing a human-interest type of story. Everything else in the news typically took precedence over a story about a grown man collecting the original Hot Wheels. I was bumped a few times over the years due to breaking news. It seemed that slow news days were the best environment for my story to be aired. It was just how it was and continues to this day. A totally free and remarkably effective form of marketing. The phone would ring almost immediately following each segment that aired and the collections started rolling in. The local TV news segments would air twice a day typically, so I was getting twice the exposure. It was genius.

The World Wide Web

Now that we have thoroughly covered and reviewed the "Grass Roots" approach to finding these rare and amazing collections on a limited budget, it is now time to shift our focus on the part of the puzzle that will cost you a fair amount of money upfront and moving forward. You cannot go into this aspect of marketing yourself in hopes of finding collections if you are not willing to spend money or are under-capitalized. By "under-capitalized", in layman's terms means, you do not have the funds to support this aspect of marketing. It can be a very costly venture in the beginning, with not only website creation and development, but also the amount of personal time you will have to sacrifice if you genuinely want to do this properly from the get-go. You must also realize that you do not create a website with all its content once and never do anything to it again. If you are going to do this correctly, you must commit funds and time to performing updates to your site on a regular basis to stay at the top of search engines. You must also always keep an eye on your competition and figure out what they are doing to capture solid leads. I choose to always respect and learn from my competitors in business and this wonderful hobby. It keeps me on my toes and keeps my competitive juices flowing. Let me put it this way and pose this question; If you were fortunate enough, and had the capital to buy into a successful franchise model, like a Chick-Fil-A or something similar, would you choose not to follow the proven business plan that is laid out for you, as a new owner, to make the most money you possibly could? I think we all know the answer to that question. If you are going to take the leap into a venture like this, learn from someone like me that has made all the costly mistakes along the way, and knows what works and what does not work after three decades of incredible and unparalleled success.

In the mid-nineties, I was contemplating a website dedicated to the Redline Hot Wheels and offering cars for sale. I was working as an athletic trainer in a large high school in southern New Jersey at the time. One of my student trainers was a young man that was incredibly knowledgeable about this new thing called the world wide web and the internet. This language to someone in my generation, for the most part, was very foreign to us. My student trainer, Mike, tried to educate me on how this was the next greatest thing in the world of business. It was the early years of the dot coms. He convinced me, over time, that he could create an eye-catching website based on the original Hot Wheels and reflective of what I was trying to accomplish in locating collections. So, I took this leap of faith into what, at the time for me, was the unknown and not well understood in the least.

Mike and I thought long and hard for not only the name of the website but also what domain we were going to purchase. We finally landed on "Hot Wheel High" and purchased the domain www.HotWheelHigh.com. The name encompassed a couple different meanings or feels to it. Was it a High School for only Hot Wheels? Was it a feeling of complete euphoria that you would get every time you laid eyes on a Hot Wheels toy car? No matter how the internet community defined it, we were fine with it. We thought it was very catchy and would attract those familiar with the toy line. Ultimately, we wanted to capture those individuals, from my generation, that still had in their possession, these highly sought after, and unbelievably valuable antique toy cars. Next, we had to come up with lots of things that would be contained within the website and what the opening scene or homepage would look like. We jotted down our ideas and thoughts and then placed them strategically into an outline.

Once we had our outline in place, we had to put our heads together and come up with an animated scene when someone visited the site. We decided on the high school theme with a souped-up Camaro burning rubber and doing a donut in front of the main entrance to the school. The Camaro had to be blue with a black roof. Mike did not quite understand my persistence until I explained to him the importance of this particular car. Mike went on to create this amazing eight second scene on the homepage when first opened. Depending on the type and speed of the computer at the time, determined how quickly the animation loaded up. I must say, looking back, it really loaded up quite quickly relative to the times.

Following the creation of the homepage's opening graphics and animation, we moved on to adding my personal bio. I was not very well known in the hobby at the time, as I typically only attended local flea markets and toy shows. It was not until I moved out west for five years that I attended my first Hot Wheels Convention in Los Angeles, California in 2016. The website needed a commerce page, or what I like to call, a section where I could sell my overflow of Redline Hot Wheels to the public. So, it was done, and I began shipping cars, not only all throughout the United States, but all around the world. I even ended up with a sailor in the Navy that was stationed on an aircraft carrier that purchased cars from me and my website. Yes, I shipped Hot Wheels to a US Naval ship back in the day. The website was multi-functional as it not only provided a platform to sell my cars, but also was primarily created to bring in more original collections. It accomplished both on a regular basis. Again, this was done on a budget as my student would not take any payment and made it a project for one of his classes that he received an "A+" on. I did make him take some money from me which I am certain put a big smile on his face.

Today's Internet

Today, the internet is a far cry from where it was twenty-five years ago when I was first introduced to it in the mid-nineties. This incredible resource and marketing tool continues to bring leads in on newly discovered original Hot Wheels collections almost on a weekly basis. Having a website is the first step in creating another piece of the puzzle in luring Hot Wheels collections to your doorstep. Purchasing a domain and creating the website is one thing, but SEO (Search Engine Optimization) is a whole other ball game, and one that must be implemented at the start, analyzed, and improved on a regular basis. You must educate yourself on many things related to your website to help drive potential visitors with Redline collections to your Contact Page, which ultimately makes your phone Ring or email "Bing." Like how I made that rhyme?

This can be a costly venture if you do not possess the knowledge or skillset to manage this oh so important aspect of your website. You will end up very frustrated by the lack of calls and emails you receive if you do not implement and maintain a solid Search Engine Optimization plan. Trust me when I tell you that I made this mistake time and time again because I really did not understand it until my web designer, the incomparable Mr. Larry Siegel, CEO of Marketing Fusion, educated me thoroughly on the topic and its importance. Larry has been with my company Geese Chasers, LLC since the early days, and remains an integral part of managing my Geese Chasers (www.GeeseChasers.com) and Redline Archeology (www.RedlineArcheology.com) websites and their SEO.

In recent years, one thing that I have learned with increasing the ranking of my website and having it show up on the first page of most internet searches, was to create meta-tags. These were words and phrases that were placed in an area that was not visible to a visitor on the homepage. They were probably the most important aspect of a website's ranking for many years. It was not until more recently when the meta-tags seem to fall out of favor with programmers and were not as vitally important in the rankings as is the SEO. The way I understand it is that the homepage and all the content throughout a site must have a flow to it with all the verbiage. Words and phrases can no longer just be popped into a paragraph or sentence anymore to check the box and increase rankings. This was a very tricky and headache producing process for me at the onset until I became more comfortable with the concept and how I would apply it to my website. A creative and eye-catching website along with a solid SEO plan with monitoring and analysis is only part of the overall online plan to produce leads with Redline Era Hot Wheels collections.

The immensely popular Redline Archeology website's homepage. Hundreds of visitors stop by each day to read the latest BLOGS and view the latest discoveries by Bob Young, Chief Redline Archeologist

The BLOG

The BLOG. Every time I hear the word it takes me back to my childhood and reminds me of the famous horror movie, The BLOB. The BLOB was a movie that had such an impact on our society and culture in the late fifties and throughout the sixties. The movie was released in 1958 and starred Steve McQueen and Aneta Corsaut. Steve McQueen was a Hollywood icon and remains a true legend to this day. The BLOB had the same impact on us as kids that the movie JAWS had in the seventies. I hope that paints a much clearer picture as to why I am reminded every time I sit down to write my next BLOG.

A friend of mine, Aaron, for years advised me to start writing a regular BLOG for my website, but it fell on deaf ears for the most part. Aaron was and still is involved in the search engine optimization aspect of internet marketing and is considered, by many, to be an expert in the field. Not sure why I didn't heed his advice sooner, but I guess I was busy with other things and truly did not understand this thing that reminded me of a very scary childhood movie.

In the winter of 2020, I finally decided to investigate this "BLOG" thing a little more and engaged Aaron in a much more detailed conversation on the benefits of adding this feature to my website. Aaron explained the BLOG theory to me in a very understandable way that started to make total sense. Keep in mind that the BLOG must be housed on a website, so that must be in place before the BLOG section can be added. I moved forward with the decision to commit to this task of writing an interesting, detailed, and fun BLOG on a regular monthly basis. One other bit of advice that Aaron passed onto me was that the search engine companies look, not only at the flow of an article (BLOG), but they also look at the length and content. BLOGs should never be too brief in length is one of the main points. Flow is another critically important aspect to each BLOG, as it was explained to me. Search engines will take all three of these vitally important aspects of a BLOG into account when deciding on the ranking and where the respective website shows up, if at all, on the first page. Keep these three things in mind when writing a BLOG: length, flow, and content.

My first BLOG was titled "Are My Old Hot Wheels Valuable?", and it ended up being an exceedingly popular and highly viewed article. Under the advice and direction from Larry Siegel, my web designer extraordinaire, I added a few high-definition pictures of Redline Hot Wheels to go with it. It changed everything. Leads were starting to flow in at an even higher rate than usual, and they were much better in quality. By quality I mean that I did not have to sift through ten emails from individuals with mainline or the newer Hot Wheels. No offense, but I only search out and collect the originals from the sixties and early seventies from when I grew up. The leads were exactly what I was hunting for, original one owner Redline Era Hot Wheels collections. I wanted to kick myself for not taking Aaron's advice sooner. Lesson learned as they say.

Other examples of BLOG topics that I have written about and placed on my website are "What are Considered the Two Rarest & Most Desirable Redline Hot Wheels?", "What is a Redline Hot Wheels?", and "What are the rarest colors of the Original Hot Wheels?" I even added an article that featured myself and two other prominent Hot Wheels collectors by an immensely popular online publication called "The HUSTLE" as one of my monthly BLOGs. The HUSTLE titled the feature "The Indiana Jones of Hot Wheels." The BLOG created on my website was titled, "Redline Archeology Featured in Recent Issue of "The HUSTLE."" So, as you can see, BLOGs do not only have to be a self-written article every time by the website's owner but can be an article written about them by a totally independent publication.

The BLOG is yet just another piece of the marketing puzzle that helps deliver leads and ultimately Redline Era Hot Wheels collections to your doorstep. I have witnessed it firsthand and am finally a believer in, da da da daaaaaaaa, THE BLOG. Coming soon to a website near you. Oh, come on, it was just hanging out there like a ripe apple.

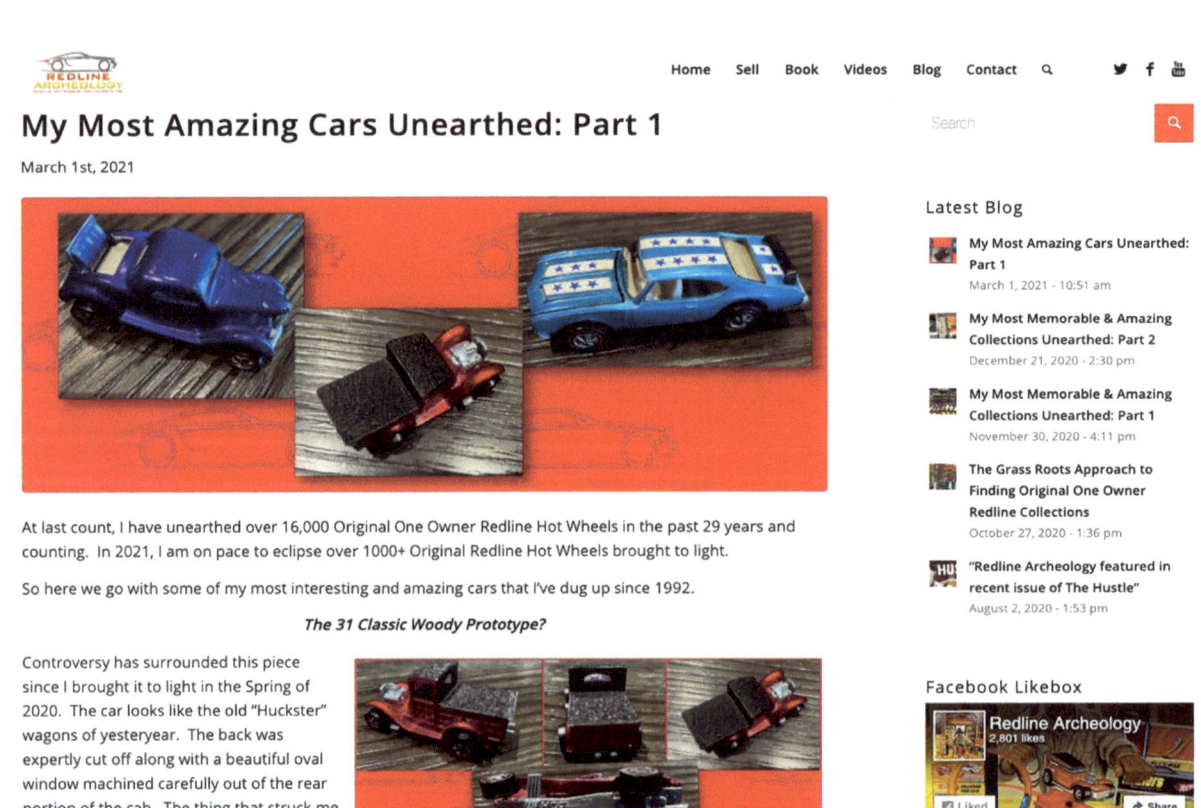

Sample Blog Entry

The YOUTUBE Channel

I must once again give total credit for this idea to my friend Aaron. Aaron talked more about this tool and aspect of search engine optimization as much as, if not more than, the Da Da Daaaaaaaaa BLOG. The YOUTUBE Channel is something that I would enjoy from time to time for "How to Fix Things" short videos, Hot Wheels Convention videos, and any other topic that piqued my interest. YOUTUBE is a great and fun way to kill some time on a slow day. This was another piece of the marketing and SEO puzzle that I should have integrated into my business plan a long, long time ago, but it is now in my rear views as they say. Also, a YOUTUBE Channel can be accomplished without a website in place, but I do not recommend this approach. You can certainly develop some leads without the website, but this is not the ideal situation to maximize your efforts. You will always get a lot more bang for your "website buck" per se if your YOUTUBE Channel has a very visible presence and placeholder on the respective homepage of your website.

So, I kicked myself again and started to create videos for my newly created Redline Archeology YOUTUBE channel back on September 3rd, 2013. It was not until the year 2016 that I started to take it seriously though and started to create and upload informative and fun videos for the hobby. Most of my early videos were, in my opinion, horrendous, so I have gone and sent most of them to the YOUTUBE Channel dumpster. Leading up to the release of my first book, **REDLINE ARCHEOLOGY "A History of Diggin' Up Original Hot Wheels Collections"**, I started to create video updates on the progress I was making and a possible release date.

The Redline Archeology YOUTUBE channel did not gain any amount of traction or steam until I posted a rare find out of Western Iowa that had a connection to a former Mattel employee of the sixties and seventies. The collection was an epic discovery and one certainly for the Redline Archeology record books. The collection totaled almost 200 cars and produced Prototypes, Early Production models, and blister pack fresh cars across the board. At that point, the views of the video started to go through the roof and subscribers were coming to the channel by the droves. To this day, the Red Oak, Iowa collection remains my most popular video with over ten thousand views and counting.

The types of videos that earn a spot on the channel are typically unveilings or unboxings of my most recent finds. I always receive, for the most part, a lot of positive feedback from Hot Wheels enthusiasts of all ages. Occasionally I will put together a video of my personal collection or a "How To" or "Informative" type of video of something related to the Redline Era of Hot Wheels. Remember that consistency plays a big role in marketing. Just like the BLOG aspect, I try to create and upload a YOUTUBE Channel video a minimum of once a month. Depending on how the Hot Wheels gods are shining down on me, usually dictates the frequency of my videos. Also, promote all your other accomplishments and any related social media outlets if you have any, during one of your videos every now and then. I always take a few moments to mention my website, first book, and my social media outlets in many of my YOUTUBE Channel videos. I will even place my first book in the background of some of my videos, and this has driven more sales of it as well. Asking viewers to LIKE each video, SUBSCRIBE to your channel, and SHARE your YOUTUBE channel with their friends and Facebook pages is also a way to generate more traffic and followers. They are all connected and will work collectively if you take the time to allow them to. This will absolutely increase your search engine optimization and traffic to levels you never dreamed, nor could pay for.

Changing it up at times adds a new look to the channel and videos. In 2020 I had the incomparable, amazing, unparalleled in his field, Mr. Carmine "Francis Ford" Cantwell, Jr. (fellow local passionate Redline Hot Wheels Collector) produce a fantastic unveiling video of an incredible collection out of Lodi, California. It was very professionally done and only cost me a few Redlines. Really nice Redlines I must say but Carmine is well worth it. He is an exceptionally talented young man, and in my opinion, has a very bright future in the film production field. I am honored that he got his start with me on the Redline Archeology YOUTUBE Channel. I also had to bribe his personal valet as well, (Carmine Sr.) with a blister pack fresh Red Baron. It was so worth it, and we are planning on doing it again when the next unbelievable collection arrives at Redline Archeology. It was and still is one of my most popular and well received YOUTUBE Channel videos, appreciated by the Redline and Hot Wheels community with positive messages, compliments, and comments I continue to receive since its release.

The YOUTUBE Channel is a vital part in generating more visitors to your website and acquiring good solid leads on collections. It is, and remains, one of my most important and highest lead producers in my marketing arsenal.

FACEBOOK

Facebook is considered the most widely used social media platform in the world, and certainly in the Redline Hot Wheels collector community. Creating and maintaining a Facebook page for your quest of searching out collections is possible without having a website, but, like YOUTUBE and other social media opportunities, it is not ideal. I strongly recommend still having a creative, cool, and understandable website that captures the attention of every visitor.

Creating and launching my Redline Archeology Facebook page was absolutely the first thing I did in conjunction with my new website build-out, Redline Archeology dot com. Immediately, and by the end of the first week, I received a private message from one of my college lacrosse teammates who told me that he still had his original Hot Wheels collection from his childhood. He went on to tell me that his wife had them tagged and ready to be sold at an upcoming yard sale she had planned for the next weekend, Saturday to be exact. You talk about timing being everything in life. This was the perfect example of being in the right place at exactly the right time. We talked about the good ole college lacrosse days before diving into his collection. Afterall, we had not seen each other or spoken for over thirty-five years.

He went on to describe a handful of the heavyweights and some more common cars that I seem to find in every collection like the Jack Rabbit Special, Paddy Wagon, and Twinmill. The collection contained approximately four dozen cars and came in a forty-eight-car stack case. I was extremely excited that my new venture into the Facebook arena and the world of social media marketing paid off instantly. It took me back to 1992 when I purchased my first twenty-four car collection on the seventh and final day of my classified ad in the Courier-Post newspaper. With the Facebook find, I was calling San Diego home at the time and was scheduled to make a trip back home to New Jersey in four weeks. We planned to meet at my house in Mt. Laurel, NJ to see the collection and do the exchange. Everything worked out as planned and I not only scored my first collection online through Facebook, but I was able to reconnect with a long-lost, college lacrosse teammate and friend. We have remained in touch ever since and he is always on the lookout for original Redline Hot Wheels for me.

Redline Archeology's immensely popular Facebook Page dedicated to everything Hot Wheels

Facebook is no different than any other social media platform regarding it being a highly effective and useful platform if used properly. Regular and consistent posting of pictures of recently discovered collections, videos of collections being unveiled, fun Redline Hot Wheels facts, Hot Wheels polls, Hot Wheels surveys, Redline sales, links to other related Hot Wheels websites, and just about anything else that is interesting to those that either "LIKE" or "FOLLOW" the page is vital to the main task at hand of attracting solid leads. Your YOUTUBE Channel should be mentioned along with a link and or one of its' popular videos a minimum of once or twice a month. This will benefit both venues and ultimately supports the main goal of what you are trying to achieve in unearthing collections. Consistently posting a link to your main website a minimum of once every two weeks is ideal and will drive more traffic to your homepage. This is a balancing act and you do not want to overdo it or keep posting the same exact thing repeatedly and too frequently, as the page will become stale, and you will potentially lose visitors and followers. This will also affect your SEO negatively if you let it.

Another way that I have found to attract more followers and build my reputation and exposure online is to have an occasional give-away with a trivia contest. At times I will award the individual with the right answer with a free autographed copy of my first book or another of many items that I have at my fingertips, including, yes, the almighty Redline. You must give to receive, and I have always been a firm believer in this, especially in the business world.

Hot Wheels collectors in general, and Redline Era Hot Wheels collectors more specifically, engage with Facebook like no other social media outlet in the world. There are literally hundreds if not thousands of Hot Wheels related pages that attract a slew of members and followers alike. New pages seem to pop up daily in this hobby and each one is just as, or more unique, than their predecessors. It is an extremely exciting and fun experience being part of the Facebook Hot Wheels community and one that appears to have many more years of life ahead.

Additional Options

There are, as they say, many ways to skin a cat. Well, in the Redline Hot Wheels collecting world, as we have discussed, there are many ways to get the word out on who you are and what you specialize in. TWITTER, INSTAGRAM, die-cast shows, Craigslist, and online antique markets are some of these additional options. Most types of social media can and will produce results at many different levels. Over time, I have collected data and tracked results from the social media outlets that I use frequently, and YOUTUBE and Facebook have always been way ahead of the pack in generating traffic to my website and producing solid leads that have allowed me to purchase some of the most amazing Redline era collections the Hot Wheels collector hobby has ever seen.

Finding original Redline Era collections can be extremely time consuming, costly, and depending on how far you take it, an extremely difficult venture to dive into. If done correctly, it can and will produce incredible results with achieving the ultimate goal of finding original Redline Era collections. My methods, strategy, and approach to searching out and unearthing these hidden gems is never static and always evolving. You must always try and remain current with the hobby and all the happenings that are taking place on a daily basis. It is truly vital to your overall success in achieving your goals. I am always looking for ways of improving and maintaining my ranking on search engines at or near the top.

The Jobby

Competition is something that you must always respect and keep an eye on. In business, I enjoy competition as it keeps me thinking all the time of what I can do better. Having business and entrepreneurial skills is a huge plus in this niche' in the hobby. You must approach this as what I like to now call a "Jobby" thanks to my dear friend Jacuveline. I truly give her one hundred percent of the credit and here is why. My wife and I were out to dinner with her and her husband, Dominic recently, and we got to talking about my passionate hobby of searching out the Redline Era Hot Wheels collections. Jacuveline and her husband Dom chuckled and she instantly blurted out, "You have a Jobby." My wife and I looked at each other and laughed out loud as we instantly realized that this was absolutely the best way to describe my thirty-year passion and love of diggin' up the Redline Hot Wheels in one simple all encompassing word. It was genius and thank you Jacuveline for your incredible grasp of the English language.

Yes, it is an extremely fun and entertaining hobby, but, if you want to achieve a high level of success in scoring these collections, you must treat it like a job. Hence, it is to me, now a "Jobby." Marketing is ongoing and needs a look outside of the box at times and on a somewhat consistent and regular basis. Branding is another vitally important aspect of growing your "Jobby" as well. I am not saying to come up with a so-called gimmick of sorts, but you must create a feel to your website, Facebook page, YOUTUBE Channel, and everything else you choose to utilize in marketing yourself. I was fortunate enough to fall into the role of the "Indiana Jones of Hot Wheels" as this is what many longtime collectors in the hobby refer to me as. It is a very identifiable and well-known character that reflects a certain feel and understanding. People in and out of the hobby understand completely what this means immediately. It really does define me and what I do in the Hot Wheels collector world.

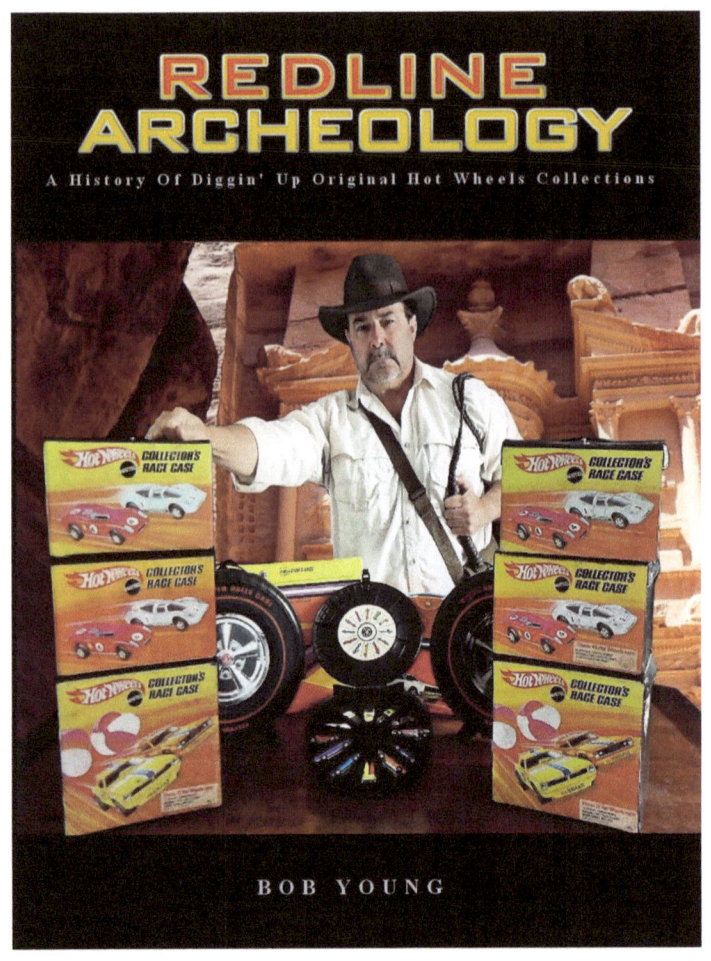

Bob Young, the Indiana Jones of the Hot Wheels collector world.

Overview of Diggin' Up Redline Collections

So, let us summarize and wrap up the conversation of the "How to Guide to Finding Original Redline Era Hot Wheels Collections." Now that we have covered, in depth, all the tools or weapons in my archeological arsenal to find these rare and amazing collections that have been in hiding for over five decades, it is now time to review and place the final red bow on this beautiful gift to every passionate Redline Hot Wheels collector that wants to experience the incredible feeling of landing an amazing Redline Era original Hot Wheels collection, in the wild, that literally has not been dusted off or seen the light of day in over five decades. I can say, with all honesty, even to this day, and hundreds of collections later, the feeling has never faded, not even a little bit when discovering an original one owner Redline Era collection of Hot Wheels. It truly is a feeling that is indescribable and one that keeps me motivated to keep doing what I love doing: diggin' up original Redline Era Hot Wheels collections. Let me put it this way; it is like hitting a "hole-in-one" for a golfer. It makes you want to keep doing what you are doing because the result and overall feeling is so indescribable and unbelievably amazing.

The Archeological Assets

If you were a baker, we would call the following a "recipe." If you were a pharmacist or mathematician, we would label it a 'formula." If you were an architect or a builder, you would refer to this as the "plan or plans." I prefer to call my methods the "Archeological Assets." So here we go:

1. **Create a cool and affordable business card that tells the complete story and is not "too busy."**

2. **Never leave home without a bunch of business cards in your pocket, never. Pass them out to anyone and everyone.**

3. **Create a cool and not "too busy" flyer that quickly and efficiently explains what you are looking for and how to get a hold of you.**

4. **Attach a few of your business cards along the border of the flyer when hanging on a cork board.**

5. **Place your flyer at eye-level and in the middle of the bulletin board. Move other business cards out of the way if you must.**

6. **Place your flyers everywhere there is an opportunity like, supermarkets, coffee shops, employee lounges, and any business where there is a community bulletin board.**

7. **Investigate the low or no-cost local and regional publications in your area and place an ad. Run the ad consistently during the times of year you determine to be best over time.**

8. **Send emails to your local affiliate news stations, TV shows, and newspapers with a short bio on the uniqueness of what you do. Sensationalize it a bit and promote the fun and unique thing that you are doing. These news outlets love to add interesting and fun human-interest stories as part of their daily or weekly repertoire.**

9. **Come up with a "brand", secure a domain, and create a website that is fun, cool, interesting, and hits the mark on who you are and what you do.**

10. **Commit to regular updates to your website.**

11. **Schedule and write an informative, fun, and interesting BLOG monthly. Add high-definition pictures to compliment every BLOG. Think about what information you would like to read about in the hobby and as a collector.**

12. **Create a YOUTUBE Channel and commit to regular videos. Make them fun, exciting, and informative for collectors. Think about what you would like to see as a collector.**

13. **Create a Facebook page with regular posts about everything Redline Era Hot Wheels.**

14. **Cross-promote and link all your social media outlets with your amazing website. Make**

sure, each one has a visible spot and placeholder on your homepage plus a quick link or icon to each respective outlet.

15. **Visit antique stores, flea markets, yard sales, garage sales, and estate sales always asking if they have any Hot Wheels or Matchbox Toy cars. Be general and keep in mind that many people still to this day think all toy cars are "Matchbox." Pass out your business card and flyer at these venues.**

So, there you have it, this precious and invaluable grouping of all my "Archeological Assets" that I utilize and apply round the clock, twenty-four hours a day, seven days a week, three hundred and sixty-five days a year. In other words, my dusty treasure map for success. I hope that every one of you gets to experience the utter joy and excitement of unearthing and scoring one of the Redline Era Hot Wheels collections in all their original and untouched beauty. It is a feeling like no other and all the sights and smells will take you back to a much simpler time in your life. I guarantee it.

Chapter 8

My Most Recent Amazing Discoveries

Over the past three years and since the release of my first book **REDLINE ARCHEOLOGY *"A History of Diggin' Up Original Hot Wheels Collections"*** in the Fall of 2018, my quest for Redline Hot Wheels collections have continued to keep me quite busy. I have purchased dozens of original collections and thousands of Redlines over the last thirty-six months. Many of these incredible finds have produced cars that not only have never been seen in the hobby before, but some discoveries were not even known to exist in the Redline Hot Wheels collector world. Eyebrows have been raised and many heads have collectively shaken when gazing upon, for the first time, some of my utterly astounding discoveries. Prototypes, early production models, test cars, paint samples, zamac cars, and some of the rarest, cleanest, and earliest examples and releases by Mattel have shown their beautiful little faces in Hot Wheels flat and stack cases on a regular basis over these last three years.

As a passionate Redline Archeologist and collector of the original and oldest Hot Wheels, I think it is vitally important to the hobby that I continue to share these amazing finds with other spirited collectors. Keeping other collectors engaged and excited about this wonderful hobby is something that we all must try to do whenever we have the opportunity. Of course, there will be those that will not support what I do or will criticize it on many levels and outlets, but it is truly their loss not to become part of this aspect of the hobby.

Finding original Redline Era Hot Wheels collections in the "wild" is a somewhat difficult task and monumental undertaking if you do decide to venture into the jungle like I do and try your luck. The rewards are well worth the tireless effort and journey when you finally do land a rare Redline Era collection. After all these thirty years of collecting, the excitement and that special feeling continues and remains the same as it was when I opened my first Hot Wheels car and Race Set way back in July of 1968.

Even after three decades of searching out the rare original Redline Hot Wheels, I still cling to all my methods on a consistent basis. Applying them and taking advantage of every conversation and opportunity that presents itself. This philosophy of collecting has, in the past and continues to this day, brought me some of the most incredible finds the hobby has ever seen.

So, let us now take a trip down memory lane on that orange track, into the loop de loop, over the Jump Ramp, under the Lap Counter, and through the Finish Gate to see what amazing original Redline Era Hot Wheels collections the **"Indiana Jones of Redline Hot Wheels"** and **"Chief Redline Archeologist, Bob Young"** (that's me) has unearthed over the last three years. Shall we.....

A snapshot of some of the collections unearthed in 2020

The Corona, CA Collection

Unearthed: 08.16.2020

As I've always said, the collections I discover out of The Golden State seem to bring me the best overall condition cars across the board, loose or blister packed. California continues to surprise me at just about every turn and in almost every find with a rare alternative color and very desirable car or cars in each collection. Also, they seem to arrive, almost every time, in blister pack or factory fresh condition as a rule. So let us get to the collection, drumroll please….. Ladies and gentlemen, I would like to introduce you all to the CORONA, California original one owner Redline Era Hot Wheels collection. Sit back and enjoy the ride on the back seat of a Rrumbler. Here we go.

The Entire Original One Owner Collection discovered in Corona, California in 2020

When this collection arrived, it certainly did not disappoint on any level. The overall condition of everything contained in the collection from the boxed accessories, race sets, blister packs, cases, buttons, and all the wonderful cars was something to behold, and made me take a few deep breaths into a paper bag while unpacking it.

The gentleman that owned the collection, when asked about the collection's provenance, explained to me that he really had not even thought about his treasured old toy cars until he read the recent article in "The HUSTLE" which featured myself and a couple other prominent collectors in the Hot Wheels world. The article was re-released recently as an "Honorable Mention" of one of the top stories of 2020 for the online publication. He said that he was intrigued by my story and background which prompted him to retrieve his beloved Hot Wheels out of storage where they have been hiding for the past fifty plus years and give me a call.

The exceedingly rare and blister pack fresh Magenta OLDS 442 found in the collection.

Like most individuals who own these collections, they initially describe the sentimental value that is attached to them. The people that I meet along the way can be remarkably interesting and entertaining at times, and this encounter was no exception. We talked about the good ole days of the sixties and seventies and shared similar stories and experiences. A few belly-laughs and chuckles were exchanged, and we got onto the business at hand.

The incredibly clean example of the Rose Pink 57 'bird in the collection.

The gentleman talked about the amount of fun he had with his Hot Wheels, especially the Snake and Mongoose set. That was his favorite. Thankfully, the set was still complete and in its original box. A very tough piece to find in this condition and complete. Even the instructions and inserts were intact. I was excited to learn more about the rest of his collection. The collection certainly did not disappoint on any level and was one of my top scores in the last three years.

This Custom Eldorado in yellow gives the impression of an over-chrome paint job.

There ended up being a total of fifty-eight Redline Hot Wheels from the years 1968 – 1971. All were in near mint to blister pack fresh condition. It also contained the most sought-after casting for this era of Hot Wheels, the OLDS 442 in MAGENTA and in factory fresh condition, complete with its star stickers perfectly applied and the rear spoiler intact. In the end, this collection was one that will go down in the Redline Archeology record books as one of the cleanest and nicest collections ever found. Here are the details of the entire collection that arrived at the offices of Redline Archeology on Saturday, August 16th, 2020:

ACCESSORIES

1. **Jump Ramp – near mint in box**
2. **Half Curve – near mint in box**
3. **Lap Counter – near mint in box**
4. **Daredevil Loop – near mint in box**
5. **Hot Wheels Club Kit in Envelope – near mint**

Race Sets

1. **Drag Race Action Set – near mint in box**
2. **Super Charger Sprint Set – near mint in box**
3. **Snake + Mongoose Drag Race Set – excellent in box**

Cases

1. **12 car Rally Case – factory fresh**
2. **24 car Flat Case – factory fresh**
3. **48 car Stack Case – factory fresh**

Rrumblers

1. **Torque Chop – near mint in blister pack**
2. **3-Squealer – near mint in blister pack**
3. **Roman Candle – near mint in blister pack**
4. **Straight Away – near mint in blister pack**
5. **Mean Machine – near mint in blister pack**

THE REDLINE Highlights

1. **OLDS 442, MAGENTA**
2. **Custom Camaro, BLUE with Black Roof + White Interior**
3. **Custom Cougar, BLUE with Blue Interior**
4. **Custom Corvette, BLUE**
5. **Custom Firebird, RED**
6. **Custom Mustang, RED with Red Interior**
7. **Custom Eldorado, YELLOW with White Interior**
8. **Custom Volkswagen, RED with White Interior**
9. **Custom Barracuda, AQUA**
10. **Custom T-Bird, AQUA**
11. **Beatnik Bandit, COPPER**
12. **Light My Firebird, ORANGE**
13. **Heavy Chevy, AQUA with White Interior**
14. **TNT Bird, AQUA**
15. **AMX II, MAGENTA**
16. **Ford J-Car, GOLD**
17. **Classic 57 'bird, ROSE PINK**

So, there you have it. This was unequivocally one of the more incredible discoveries in recent years out of the Golden State of California. As I always say, there is still plenty more where this one came from, and I am about to show you some more. Fasten your seatbelts as we are just getting started on this incredible journey into the world of REDLINE ARCHEOLOGY. Short Round, prepare the Jeep and pack your bags. We are headed three thousand miles east to the City of Brotherly Love for the once in a Redline Collector's lifetime find, the mind-boggling SOUTH PHILLY Collection. Maestro, find as many drums as possible for this one please….

The SOUTH PHILLY Collection
Unearthed: 12.16.2018

The phone rang, my iPhone of course, not the wall hung one I usually talk about, in mid-December 2018, and on the other end of the line was a nice, younger woman who asked me if I would be interested in looking at a box of old Hot Wheels that her deceased grandfather had just left her and her husband. She stated that she did not know anything about them, just that her grandfather purchased the cars directly from Mattel many years ago.

Hmmmmm, I was thinking that this was probably a case of modern day "Mainline Hot Wheels" that were worth about a dollar each, but I always dig a little deeper in hopes that this might be that one in a million case of rare Redline Era Hot Wheels I have been trying to hunt down for the past three decades. Well, this time I was so thankful that I did not immediately dismiss this as one of the many calls I get every week. A lot of callers have the newer stuff that I do not collect and know truly little about. The only thing I know about the newer Hot Wheels is that you can find them in just about every retail store in America and abroad hanging on pegs or stuffed in big bins. That is basically where my knowledge begins and ends with the modern-day releases.

The cordial and friendly woman went on to tell me that they had shopped the cars around locally but had some not so friendly or positive encounters with a few local toy collectors and antique dealers. She went on telling me that the last guy that came to their house became very belligerent when she and her husband would not accept his low-ball offer of eight-hundred dollars for the entire box and its contents. She stated that she and her husband knew enough to protect themselves from getting taken full advantage of in this situation. She was frustrated and just wanted to know the truth of what she possessed. I asked her to take some pictures of the box and cars contained within. She took a couple pictures of the box and one overhead shot of the top opening where you could see the cars all pressed against each other in their respective blister packs. Upon receiving the pictures on my iPhone, saying that I almost passed out was the understatement of the century. What my two eyeballs were looking at was something, as a passionate Redline collector, I had only dreamt about hundreds of times over the years. There it was, in all her glory, a 1970 original shipping case of Hot Wheels stuffed to the brim. Hold on, I just got a little light-headed re-living the moment. There, I am feeling much better now. I asked her to gently pull a few cars out and tell me their names that appeared on the metal button to the right of each car. She proceeded to name two Boss Hosses and one Nitty Gritty Kitty. This was astounding and all the information I needed. Next step was for me to try and schedule a comfortable meeting place for both of us so that I could see this incredible original case of Hot Wheels from the Redline Era. I tried to gain my composure, wiped the sweat from my brow, took a few deep breaths and gathered my thoughts before trying to discuss a time and place to meet. I did not want to sound too excited, but it was literally and totally impossible for this passionate Redline collector. I am sure that my voice was a bit shaky and quivering when I asked if we could work on a time and place to meet. Keep in mind, we were about two weeks away from Christmas and I am sure that they could have used a little extra money for the holiday season. We talked for a few minutes, her husband got on the phone with me as well and decided to invite me over to their home a couple of days later. He came off as a profoundly serious guy who was also extremely frustrated with this case of old Hot Wheels. I got the sense that he was becoming more and more skeptical with any collector coming over to see the case because of their multiple recent bad experiences with others who tried to steal or low-ball this piece of Mattel history. I did not sleep for the next two days thinking about everything else that might be contained in this, what appeared to be a complete case of ninety-six original Redline Era Hot Wheels. Of course, any true impassioned collector in my shoes would have had the same thoughts that I did of this rare find being sold to someone else prior to the scheduled meeting. Yes, over the years, and as a collector and buyer of the Redline Era Hot Wheels, this has happened to me before. Collections have been sold right out from under me and sometimes even after I submitted my thorough appraisal and generous offer. I was determined not to let it happen again, especially with this original case. Trust me, I was not going crazy or losing my mind thinking these thoughts. Well, maybe just a little.

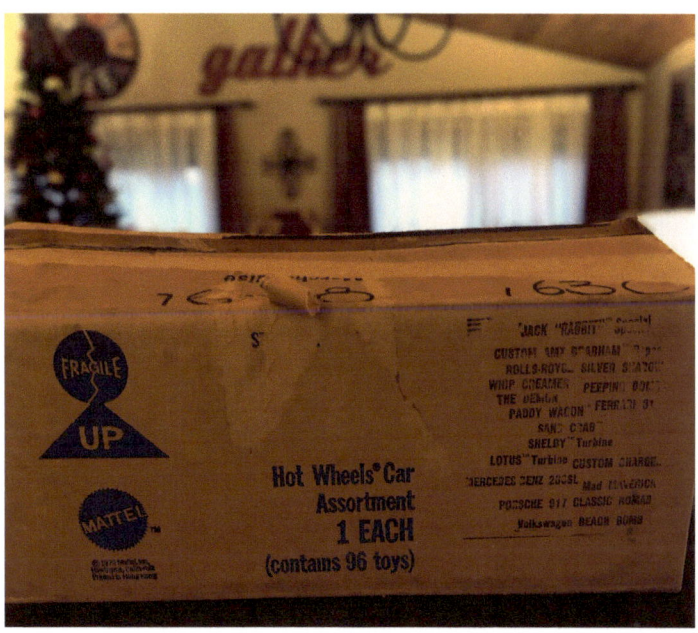

The incredible find in South Philly. An original case of 84 blister packs from 1970 ordered directly from Mattel.

The day had arrived, yet the clock seemed to be working against me as the seconds and minutes felt like they were in slow motion. The sand in my hourglass seemed to be stuck. South Philly is a place that I am very familiar with having grown up just across the Walt Whitman Bridge in Southern New Jersey. One thing I know and understand about the City of Philadelphia is parking. Parking is always an issue in these South Philly neighborhoods and throughout most of the city. Row home after row home line the narrow streets all throughout that area of the city. I grabbed my good friend Matty, who accompanied me on many of my meetings like Todd did back in the day, and we were off. I left myself a little extra time if I could not find a legal parking spot close enough and had to walk. I was even willing to incur one of the infamous Philadelphia Parking Authority tickets if I had to on this glorious day. Nothing was keeping me from an opportunity to see and possibly purchase this unbelievably rare piece of Mattel Hot Wheels history.

It was a cloudy and somewhat rainy day, but I was motivated to try and finagle a parking spot close enough, so we did not get soaked either coming or going. Especially if I were to land this potentially amazing score, I certainly did not want to have it exposed to the elements for too long. Astoundingly, Matty and I found a somewhat legal parking spot just around the corner from our designated meeting place. With lots of experience over the years with South Philly, I knew what I could and could not get away with as far as parking a vehicle was concerned. I kind of sort of parked my FJ Cruiser on a corner with part of a parking space on the corner of a street. Oh well, I did not care if I got a ticket, was towed to the PPA lot, or angered a local. Been there and done that is all I have to say. We exited the car and made our way a block and a half to the gates of, what felt like, Hot Wheels Heaven. We were smack-dab in the middle of South Philly surrounded by little Italian delicatessens, corner bars, and lots and lots of row homes. I did have a sizable amount of cash on hand at the time and had to be "street-smart" for that brief walk in the city. You learn your "street-smarts" very quickly and sometimes through bad experiences when you spend time in these major urban centers. We arrived safely at the doorstep of this typical South Philly row home, and were greeted by the friendly woman who invited us in. Introductions were made and the time was quickly approaching as I could sense the cars were just waiting to meet me. Well, if this story has not grasped your full attention yet, you better grab your favorite drink, have a seat, and dig in because here comes the best part. An experience and find that rarely surfaces in the hobby, ever.

My first look at this once in a collector's lifetime find. The Original Case of 1970 Hot Wheels.

So Matty and I walked in and were instructed to go to the kitchen where the case was awaiting our arrival. So, we walked through the family room, passed the steps to the left and dining room to the right where the decorated Christmas tree was standing proudly, and ended up in this small yet inviting typical South Philly kitchen. By a typical South Philly kitchen, I mean that everything was very well organized yet packed with fresh loaves of Italian bread, vegetables, spices, and anything else that was available at the local and incredibly famous Italian Market. You know, where "Rocky" ran through and was cheered on by all the street vendors in the first movie. I guess you must be familiar with the South Philly culture to understand.

There it was in all its glory. A basically undisturbed case of Redline Hot Wheels from 1970 still in the original box with all the inserts. I had to take a couple minutes to gather my thoughts and level off my breathing and heart rate, but I finally composed myself so I could articulate the English language in an understandable way. You think I am joking, but I truly am not. This was a moment unlike any other that I have had the honor and privilege of experiencing in this hobby or realm. Yes, I have unearthed collections that certainly rivaled this one in their own special way, but this was a packed original case from 1970. That is absolutely and undeniably correct, I said 1970!!

I asked very politely if I could take the blister packs out of the case and she obliged and instructed me to "go for it." I proceeded to remove one blister pack very gently at a time which equated into at least thirty seconds to extract one. I was being extremely careful yet trying to be efficient at the same time. It was becoming very apparent to me that this was the find of the decade. Black roof Spoilers started to show themselves to me in "runs." By the word "runs" I mean multiples in a line-up.   One after the other after the other. At this point I had only removed around ten cars in their blister packs, but I could not believe what I was looking at. It was a sight that Redline Collector dreams are made of.

The 84 cars in their blister packs contained within the 1970 original shipping case directly from Mattel.

After about thirty minutes, I had finally organized every blister pack by casting, color, roof color, interior color, and condition. I had a monumental task ahead of me that could potentially set a record for me for a purchase price of an original collection. I pulled out my daily planner and got right to cataloging each car. Matty was extremely helpful as we organized the cars by casting and color. Once I had the final total down of each casting, it was time to initiate the appraisal process. Total count of cars in their respective blister packs that were contained within the original shipping case was eighty-four. Eighty-four of the most beautiful blister pack Redline Hot Wheels that I have ever seen in one place, and they were within my grasp. To this day, even when the topic of this find comes up in conversation, I still find myself shaking my head and smiling as I begin talking about it.

One of the many Black Roof and White Interior Blister Packs discovered in the 1970 original case.

It was now imperative that I appraise the collection completely and thoroughly before making, what I always consider, my most generous and reasonable offer. The clock was ticking so I got right to it, scribbling away each car, in order, with my evaluation on condition, casting, color, and value. All my appraisals take everything into account when calculating an individual car and collection's overall value, so that I can make the most accurate estimate based on all the factors, and then base my offer upon that. My offers are typically received with wide eyes, a smile from ear to ear, a laugh or chuckle, and the proverbial "I cannot believe these cars are worth that?" type of remark. It happens almost every time with every collection I appraise and attempt to purchase. It was time to get to work and get this done without wasting anyone's time, especially the sellers.

One of the many Spoilers in multiples with White Interiors discovered in the 1970 original case.

A couple of things became very apparent to me as I was going through the entire case and all the cars. I realized that most were unpunched and in factory fresh condition. It was as if this was the first time, they were ever taken out of the shipping case that they were first placed in over 5 decades earlier. The woman explained that her grandfather would take a car or two out for her father's birthdays and again at Christmas for him and his brother, her uncle, to give as gifts to the best of her recollection from what her father explained to her. This would certainly explain the missing twelve cars that would have completed the case. These original cases held ninety-six cars in their blister packs when they shipped to all the retail stores back in the sixties and seventies. The Mattel factory would also stamp, in black ink, each of the models that were supposedly contained within, directly on the outside of the case. We will cover this later as this proved to be a shocking moment for me as well.

I finally completed my appraisal, explained to the owners the most valuable cars in the collection, and then nervously presented my more than magnanimous offer. Right at that moment, the woman's husband walked in the house and made a "B" line to the kitchen. I guess for a moment I felt that the "B" stood for me and this guy was immediately checking me and my buddy Matty out as soon as he laid eyes on us. To say that this guy was an ominous and intimidating figure would be a gross understatement. This guy stood about six feet four inches, tattoos covered both arms, and appeared to have an attitude. Even before introducing himself, he started to talk about his experience with a couple of collectors or buyers that came before me. It was not a comfortable conversation to say the least and I had to find a way to defuse the situation. He went on to say how he almost physically tossed the last guy out of the house when he would not take no for an answer. It was obvious that their experiences with buyers over the past couple of weeks did not go well, and I think I was sort of paying a price for it, for the moment anyway. In my calm, sincere way, and approach, I assured him that I was a very fair and reasonable individual that always paid a high percentage of the true value of these vintage Hot Wheels. The moment I verbalized my offer and pulled out a stack of hundred-dollar bills, all the angst and frustration seemed to leave his large intimidating body. I was relieved on so many levels. The tension was immediately swept out of the room.

My offer was met with excitement, joy, laughter, and some tears as well. They both could not believe the amount of money I was willing to pay for these toy cars in a cardboard box. They accepted my offer immediately and told me that I had just made their Christmas extra special for them and their kids. It instantly made me get even more into the holiday spirit and made me feel so much better about what I had just purchased. Matty and I carefully packed up the cars as the woman and her husband counted the money. I always ask the sellers to count the agreed upon money in front of me before I leave with any collection. It has always served me well and is a good common practice when doing these types of deals that require thousands of dollars. Matty and I said our good-byes and exited, in the pouring rain, hurriedly to our awaiting chariot. I did everything to keep even one drop of H2O from hitting this exceptional case of 1970 Hot Wheels. I did not care how soaking wet I or Matty suffered because this amazing original case of Hot Wheels from 1970 was my priority at the time. Matty and I high fived the entire way home, giggling in utter amazement at what sat on his lap. It felt as though the tires of the FJ Cruiser did not even contact the asphalt road the entire way home. We basically floated home across the Walt Whitman bridge and back into the Garden State. The feeling was truly that incredible.

I got home and placed the case on the table behind our couch and just stared at it in disbelief. I just knew that at any moment I was going to awaken from this incredible dream. My adrenaline was still running high hours and days after this extraordinary experience. Matty and I went out to dinner that night at our favorite local Italian restaurant to celebrate this once in a lifetime find. What happened the next day with this collection I am going to have to chalk up to either my adrenaline or my age. Most likely my age.

The next day I awoke to this beautiful original case of 1970 Hot Wheels in my family room on the coffee table. Still shaking my head in disbelief, I sat down and calmly started going through each of the cars. I must have sat there for two hours but enjoyed every moment. I carefully placed each of the eighty-four blister packs back in their respective spots and I went on to just take a quick look at the outside of the case for the production date. Just something I always do with the blister packs, race sets, and accessories. As I was looking around the outside of the box, I noticed all the cars' names that were stamped on its one side. It was no big deal until, drumroll please maestro, there it was in all its faded glory. The name of one of the rarest cars never sent into full production by Mattel due to legal issues, the MAD MAVERICK. The Topper Company had beaten Mattel to the name MAD MAVERICK as part of their line of Johnny Lightning cars that competed directly with the Hot Wheels line. Mattel lost the legal battle and history will tell you that the name was changed to the MIGHTY MAVERICK in lieu of the disputed name of MAD MAVERICK. One can only imagine if there was a MAD MAVERICK in the case originally packed and sent and was given out by the original owner to one of his kids. I guess we will never know but it is an interesting thing to ponder. We can now refer to this as the "Case of the Missing MAD MAVERICK." I kind of like that. It does have a catchy tune to it.

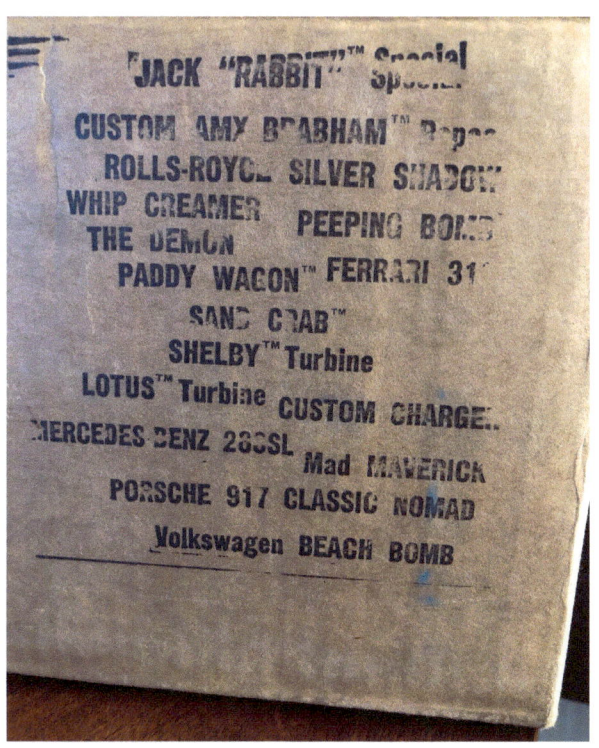

The MAD MAVERICK case of original 1970 Hot Wheels.

The MAD MAVERICK stamp up close and personal.

This was most definitely the highlight of 2018 and rivaled all my discoveries over the past thirty years. Who knows if this find will ever be repeated? I guess I will leave it up to you, the reader, to decide as we continue down this dusty dirt road of my most amazing Redline Hot Wheels discoveries over the last three years. Now if I can only find "Short Round" to lend me a hand while I lay out all the cars contained in this amazing discovery. With or without "Short Round," ladies and gentlemen, I would like you all to give a hearty welcome and the well-deserved standing ovation, to the stars of the SOUTH PHILLY Collection:

BLISTER PACKS

1. **BOSS HOSS:** (1) OLIVE - Black Roof + White Interior
   (5) COPPER – 3 White Interior, 2 Dark Interior
   (7) AQUA – 6 Black Roof + White Interior, 1 Black Roof + Dark Interior

2. **NITTY GRITTY KITTY:** (4) RED – 1 White Interior, 3 Dark Interior
   (8) BLUE – Dark Interior
   (11) AQUA – 7 White Interior, 4 Dark Interior

3. **LIGHT MY FIREBIRD:** (2) BLUE – Dark Interior
   (3) GREEN – Dark Interior
   (3) OLIVE – Dark Interior

4. **TNT BIRD:** (2) OLIVE – 1 White Interior, 1 Dark Interior
   (5) BLUE – Dark Interior
   (5) RED – Dark Interior

5. **CUSTOM CHARGER:** (3) RED

6. **MERCEDES 280sl:** (1) ORANGE
   (1) COPPER
   (2) PURPLE
   (2) RED
   (2) GREEN

7. **CUSTOM CONTINENTAL MK IV:** (1) MAGENTA
   (4) LIME YELLOW

8. **BRAHBAM REPCO F1:** (2) PURPLE
   (2) AQUA

9. **SHELBY TURBINE:** (4) BLUE
   (3) ORANGE
   (1) GREEN

You may be seated! I warned you how inconceivable a find this was and one that may never come around again in the hobby. I never say never and keep my fingers crossed that another case is just around the corner. Can anyone say 1968? I know you were thinking that as well.

Short Round, fuel the engine on our prop plane. We have a full day's flight ahead of us as we head west approximately twenty-eight hundred miles to the town of El Dorado Hills, California, just outside the state's capitol of Sacramento. Fasten your seat belts… What was that Short Round? Oh, right, there are no seat belts. Oh well, brace yourself for the bumpy ride ahead to the Golden State.

The EL DORADO HILLS, CA Collection
Unearthed: 01.19.2019

At the time, I was still living on the west coast in San Diego when this unexpected collection presented its beautiful self to me. I received an email from my website's "Contact Page" from a young man who said that his grandmother came across a bunch of old Hot Wheels in their original package and needed help with their individual and overall values. I, as always, obliged but had some questions I needed answered first. I do receive a lot more inquiries of the newer stuff than I do the Redlines. As they say, you must kiss a lot of frogs before finding that prince, or in my case, that princess. Not that the other Hot Wheels are frogs, but they are not what I search out in my quest to find the rarest of the Hot Wheels, the Redlines.

I went ahead and passed my questions onto the grandson and he was acting as an intermediary or liaison for his grandmother. I asked that she look on the back of the blister packs and identify the year of production and place of origin. Getting just the year of production is not enough as a lot of models have been reproduced over the years and still express a production year as far back as 1967. Gathering this information determines if I am going to get off the Redline Express or continue with gathering the ever-important provenance. She provided all the necessary information to her grandson, and it was confirmed that these were the originals from the sixties and seventies. Now I was starting to pay much closer attention and get a bit more excited. My next steps were to request pictures of all the cars in question. The grandson told me he lived over an hour away from his grandmother and where the cars were stored, so it might be a few days before he could get up there to photograph them and text message me the pictures.

A couple of weeks went by and I had not heard back from the gentleman. I decided to place a call to him to see if the collection was still in play. I try to never bother someone but at the same time did not want to lose the opportunity of possibly purchasing this potentially rare collection. It is a balancing act but a tightrope that you must walk successfully if you want to stay in the good graces of the seller. He apologized emphatically that he did not get back to me sooner. He went on to explain that his grandmother was taken ill for a spell but was now feeling better. He also stated that he was headed up there the following weekend to get some pictures of the cars for me to view. He was a man of his word and right on time, the pictures started popping up on my cell phone via text message that Saturday morning. Text messaging, as I have said, is always the easiest and most understandable way of attaining pictures from the sellers. Picture after picture was gracing my phone and they did not disappoint, except for the fact, when I took a much closer look, they all had the top half of their cards cut off. They are what we call in the hobby as "Cut Cards."

The 48 Cut Card blister pack collection with some exceptionally clean and rare Redlines.

Now the real work began, so I sharpened my pencil and got right to it. My initial step when I receive a group photo of an entire collection like this one, whether loose or carded, is to take a first look to see what the rarest and most desirable pieces are, and request additional individual photos of those I identify as the cream of the crop. I immediately got to it and made a list of the cars that I wanted additional, high definition, in focus, and well-lit pictures of. The gentleman accommodated my request and sent me all the pictures I wanted and in focus.

In the meantime, I was gathering the provenance on the forty-eight-cut carded Redlines and was a bit surprised by what I heard about the cards being halved by his grandfather, the original owner.

He said that he had spoken to his grandmother regarding this, and she replied, when asked the question on why the cards had been cut, she replied "My husband wanted to store them safely in our wooden chest in our bedroom at the foot of our bed where we kept our linens and comforters. He ended up cutting each of the cards in half to save room for storage purposes." Well, there you have it. The blister packs were cut in half to reduce the overall size necessary to store all forty-eight cards. Like I always say, there is usually a method to everyone's madness, and this was theirs.

When valuing cut cards or blister packs, it is a given in the Redline world that any cards that have been either damaged, ripped, or cut, the value is basically on the car only as a loose piece. In my world, I appraise cut or damaged blister packs as loose cars. I know that there are many collectors in this hobby that would agree with me since anyone that purchases one of these cut cards typically removes the car from it and places it on display in their respective collection. Most cars that come out of damaged or cut cards are usually in near mint to factory fresh condition, so this usually makes the most sense.

Four hot pink, cut card blister packs of some very desirable pieces in factory fresh condition. The Power Pad, Seasider, Custom Eldorado with white interior, and Custom AMX.

My appraisal was completed within a couple of days due to a minor delay in receiving a few extra photos of some of the higher end cars. I just wanted to be sure that there were not any surprises like, paint toning, paint rubs on the inside of the plastic blister, and missing sticker sheets where applicable. I completed the appraisal and presented my offer to the gentleman, and he relayed it immediately to his grandmother. To say they were exceedingly happy with my offer would be to trivialize it. She requested to speak with me after all this time had gone by to thank me for my time, knowledge, patience, and indulgent offer.

Two rare cars, the brown Hot Heap and Beachbomb along with the red Mighty Maverick. All very desirable pieces in the Redline world.

She was so happy with the deal and went on to explain to me how comfortable I made her, and her grandson feel the entire time. This type of feedback and experience I have with owners of these rare collections is what further reinforces my philosophy on how I approach this aspect of the "Hunt." Positive feedback is always a welcome and pleasant thing to receive on my end. Makes me feel good about the way I do things in this wonderful hobby of ours.

Three very desirable cars that are part of the "Spoiler Series", the green Light My Firebird, blue Boss Hoss, and orange with white interior Heavy Chevy.

The cars arrived a few days later safe and sound to my home in San Diego and I could not have been more pleased with the collection. All the cars showed up in the exact way they were depicted in the hundreds of photos I received from the owner's grandson. Kudos to him for a job very well done. Unbelievably, another heart-stopping discovery out of California. California may be the avocado capital of the world, but boy does it keep kicking out tons of beautiful Redline Era Hot Wheels collections, one after the other, for this happy Redline Archeologist. I propose that we change the slogan of the state to "The Spectraflame State." Thoughts?

Ok Short Round, let us get to the part where we introduce all the fine additions to our growing collection from the Eldorado Hills, CA original one owner Redline Era Hot Wheels collection. Drumroll please Maestro….. Ladies and gentlemen, please stand and give all of these beautiful pieces of Mattel history a rousing round of applause and warm welcome….. Give it up for…. The ELDORADO HILLS, CALIFORNIA All-Stars:

1. Tri-Baby, PURPLE
2. Red Baron
3. Hairy Hauler, RED
4. Splittin' Image, LITE BLUE
5. The Demon, BLUE
6. Indy Eagle, AQUA
7. Ferrari 312p, RED ENAMEL
8. Lotus Turbine, RED
9. Brahbam Repco F1, BLUE
10. Ford Mk IV, RED ENAMEL
11. Ford J-Car, PURPLE
12. Porsche 917, HOT PINK
13. Shelby Turbine, GREEN
14. Classic Nomad, YELLOW
15. Custom Continental Mk IV, AQUA
16. Fire Chief Cruiser
17. Carabo, GREEN with White Interior
18. Silhouette, AQUA with White Interior
19. Jack Rabbit Special
20. Swingin' Wing, ROSE PINK
21. Beatnik Bandit, AQUA
22. Maserati Mistral, RED
23. Mercedes 280sl, BLUE
24. Light My Firebird, GREEN
25. Boss Hoss, BLUE
26. Heavy Chevy, ORANGE with White Interior
27. Nitty Gritty Kitty, RED with White Interior
28. TNT Bird, RED
29. Sugar Caddy, BLUE
30. Mantis, ROSE PINK
31. Classic '36 Ford Coupe, AQUA with White Interior
32. Classic '32 Ford Vicky, GOLD with White Interior
33. Classic '31 Ford Woody, GOLD with White Interior
34. Custom Corvette, AQUA White Interior
35. Custom Charger, BLUE
36. Power Pad, HOT PINK
37. Seasider, HOT PINK
38. Custom Eldorado, HOT PINK with White Interior
39. Custom AMX, HOT PINK
40. Turbofire, RED
41. Grass Hopper, APPLE GREEN
42. Classic '57 -Bird, RED with White Interior
43. Hot Heap, BROWN
44. Mighty Maverick, RED
45. Beachbomb, BROWN
46. Snake, YELLOW
47. Mongoose, RED
48. Whip Creamer, LIME YELLOW

Ok, you may now be seated. Take some deep breaths as we are only getting started. "Short-Round, prepare the next discovery please and warm up the engines on the plane." We now head back east, twenty-seven-hundred miles and close to our nation's capital to the "State for Lovers" and the town of Arlington, Virginia. Here we go…..

The ARLINGTON, VA Collection
Unearthed: Independence Day, 2020

It is always so refreshing for me to unearth a collection from one of the mid-Atlantic states that has all basically blister pack fresh cars contained within. This part of the country, for me, has produced some incredible cars and collections over the years, but paint toning always seems to be a consistent problem that I run into. Homes on the east coast are typically older and have attics, basements, and garages where most of these cars are stored their entire lives. Typically, a lot of these discoveries have not seen the light of day for, in some cases, over fifty years.

This collection, however, was the exception to the rule. Seeing pictures in email and on your cell phone through text messaging is one thing, but holding them in your hand and inspecting them up close can sometimes reveal some surprises, and some not in a good way. Upon receiving the cars on our nation's "Day of Independence", July 4th, it gave me yet another reason to celebrate. The cars were spectacular across the board and much better in person. I was pleasantly surprised and shocked a bit considering the climate that this collection was stored in for the last five decades.

The incredibly blister pack fresh assembly of forty-nine cars out of Arlington, VA.

Forty-nine Redline Hot Wheels surrounded by their respective collectors' buttons.

The provenance of the collection was that it was an original one owner and placed in storage in 1971 never to be seen again until recently, as per the owner. We talked about growing up during this time of the Redline Era Hot Wheels and shared some similar stories. The owner reminisced about how, if he was good in school and at home during the week, he was always rewarded, by his parents, with going down to the local F.W. Woolworth Company store to pick out his reward. It was always a Hot Wheels car and sometimes he was allowed to pick out two if he had an exceptionally stellar week at school and home. He expressed how excited he was as a young boy and could not wait for that moment every week. Well, there were a few missed opportunities he went on to explain, but I think we all understand the meaning of that from being a child of the sixties.

Just an example of the quality of the overall condition of a small grouping of cars, purple Custom Volkswagen, rose pink Corvette with white interior, orange Custom AMX, and hot pink AMX II. All in factory fresh condition.

The uniqueness of the overall condition of this collection from a region that normally produces some cars with darkening or toning in a few cars' paint, was what made this collection so memorable to me as a longtime collector. Final count was forty-nine Redline Hot Wheels, 1 lonely Johnny Lightning, 39 collector buttons, and a forty-eight-car stack case. When asked about the race sets and accessories, the gentleman replied, "They probably were thrown out years ago." A much too often reply in my world. I guess the cars were a lot tougher to dispose of as compared to the orange track and accessories by our parents.

The nicest condition OLDS 442 I have ever found over the years.

The incredibly tough purple Whip Creamer in blister pack fresh condition. This one has found a home in my personal collection. Words I rarely utter.

Now comes the other amazing piece of this story out of Arlington, VA. A car showed up in this collection that I, along with many longtime and knowledgeable Redline Hot Wheels collectors, have never heard of or let alone seen in person. The funny thing about this aspect of the story is that I did not even pick up on it until a month later. I had already made the YOUTUBE video on my REDLINE ARCHEOLOGY Channel of the official unveiling of the collection and totally missed it. Yes, I missed what ended up being one of the rarest finds in my thirty-year career.

While going through my personal collection and organizing and dusting off some of my cars, I pulled this car from my tall, former rotating watch display to show a collector friend who was looking for a nice PURPLE Classic '36 Ford Coupe. I pulled it out and when I went to hand it over to him, BOOM, it punched me in the face.

There it was, right in front of me in my now shaking hand staring back at me with a "Cheshire Cat" smile. I know, I have some imagination, but that is exactly how it felt at that exact moment when I first realized what this piece actually was. It initially appeared to be a run of the mill PURPLE Classic '36 Ford Coupe to me and again, I missed it totally and completely. I have no excuses as to why I made this potentially catastrophic and epic mistake. Tsk tsk tsk and shame on me for missing it. Yes, it absolutely was a PURPLE Classic '36 Ford Coupe, but it held some secrets until now. At closer inspection there were three amazing and unique things that smacked me in the face like an apple pie. First and foremost, it had a white interior which is somewhat rare in its own right. I then noticed that its roof was unpainted and the rumble seat in the back had a light purple finish to it. I immediately got on the phone to a couple deeply knowledgeable Redline collectors I know and sent pictures to each of them. They all agreed that the car was an early test run or prototype. They also added that they had never seen or heard of one like this before in all their years of collecting the Redline Hot Wheels. Have you ever stumbled across a significant Christmas or birthday present that your parents totally forgot to give you? Well, I think you get the point. What an amazing find in an utterly amazing collection.

The never seen before Prototype purple '36 Ford Coupe with white interior, non-painted roof, and light purple rumble seat.

Now it is time to single out, identity, and give our respects to the "Top Dogs" in the Arlington, Virginia original one owner Redline Era Hot Wheels collection. Here they are, in no particular order, the ALL-STARS of the Arlington, Virginia collection:

1. **Classic '36 Ford Coupe, PURPLE with White Interior + Lite Purple Rumble Seat**
2. **OLDS 442, YELLOW**
3. **Whip Creamer, PURPLE**
4. **Custom Volkswagen, PURPLE**
5. **Custom Corvette, ROSE PINK with White Interior**
6. **Custom AMX, ORANGE**
7. **AMX II, HOT PINK**
8. **Heavy Chevy, GREEN with White Interior**
9. **TNT Bird, AQUA with White Interior**
10. **Nitty Gritty Kitty, RED with White Interior**
11. **King Kuda, OLIVE**

So, there you have it. All the kings of the collection and all in factory fresh condition. An exceedingly rare collection by any standards. It is now time for each of you to jump into your chosen concept car or custom and follow Short Round and me three thousand miles west. We now find ourselves back in the Golden State in the central and coastal part in the charming town of San Luis Obispo, California. Short Round, check the weather and wind speeds and prepare for take-off. Introducing the astonishing find out of San Luis Obispo, California.....

The SAN LUIS OBISPO, CA Collection
Unearthed: 08.22.2020

This collection was one of the more sizable ones in comparison to all the others over the last three years of diggin'. The total amount of Redline Hot Wheels was one hundred and twenty-seven, with twenty-two of them still in their blister packs. There were also three Sizzlers that showed up along with all the metal and plastic collector buttons that went with each car. Four Hot Wheels Racing World Magazines also were part of this stunning collection.

I was contacted by the original owner of this breath-taking assortment of Redlines in August 2020, almost immediately following the release of "The Hustle" online article. He told me that he subscribes via email to "The Hustle" and receives weekly issues from the publication. I personally had never heard of this online publication until I was contacted by one of the writers a month earlier who lives in San Francisco. What I did not realize was the impact that this online publication had in driving individuals to not only my website, but also to my YOUTUBE

Channel and Facebook page. The response was absolutely incredible, and I ended up with multiple collections over the next four weeks. One of the collections actually had a connection to a former Mattel employee who worked at the Hawthorne, California location in the sixties and seventies. We will get to that heart-pounding discovery later. For now, let us continue with the discovery at hand.

The San Luis Obispo, CA entire collection of 106 loose Redlines, 22 blister packs, 106 collector buttons, and 4 Club Kit Magazines.

The owner of this large and complex collection told me that he had not given it much thought until he read the article about the Hot Wheels "Whales", or collectors in this case. This prompted him to go and retrieve his old Hot Wheels out of his storage unit where they had been for literally decades. He went on to tell me that the cars were put away, in their cases, and placed in large cardboard boxes and basically forgotten about until most recently. When asked about the provenance of the collection, he told me that he was the original owner and enjoyed them immensely during his childhood growing up in California.

The beautiful US Custom Camaro in blue with a white interior flanked by a red Sugar Caddy and white enamel Snake.

Growing up in California, as this gentleman described, in the sixties and seventies, Hot Wheels were the most popular new boys' toy of its day. Created in California and spread like wildfire throughout the country and abroad at warp speed. He went on to tell me how his mother and father would surprise him on a fairly regular basis with at least a car or two. This went on for years, which was very apparent to me with the number of cars and other items contained within the collection.

The rare and very desirable hot pink with white interior Porsche 917 on the card.

There seemed to be a little sentimental value to this owner, but he said that he wanted the collection to go to someone like me that would not only appreciate the cars but would also get them in the hands of other passionate collectors. Looking back on the deal, he, like most original owners of the Redline Era Hot Wheels, wanted to spend a few more final moments with his beloved and treasured toy cars. I never rush anyone during the appraisal, negotiations, or final deal. I would feel extremely bad if someone ever felt obligated or rushed to sell me their collection. Sellers' remorse is something I try to avoid at all costs.

Pictures were sent to my iPhone of each car, blister pack, and magazine, and I got busy on evaluating it all. The overall size of this collection caused me to take an extra day to complete the appraisal. I finally wrapped up the appraisal two days later and placed a call to the owner. He was sounding a bit apprehensive about letting his prized and precious childhood toys go that he obviously cherished and held near and dear to his heart. We talked for awhile and I, as always, tried to explain to him to not sell the collection if there was still even a hint of sentimentality attached to it. He really appreciated me saying that and asked if he could just spend the upcoming weekend with the cars one last time before possibly saying his final goodbye. I absolutely agreed and told him to take as much time as he needed or wanted and reinforced that he was never to feel one ounce of obligation to sell the collection to me.

Three beautiful and desirable pieces found in the San Luis Obispo, CA Collection. The olive with black roof and white interior Custom Cougar, US blue with white interior Custom Corvette, and the lite blue Python.

The weekend came and went, and my phone rang late in the day the following Monday. The owner of the collection was on the other end of the phone and sounded in much better spirits than the last time we had spoken a week prior. He said that the weekend was all that he needed to spend with his cars, and he was ready to hear and entertain my offer. As usual, I educated him on the collection, which he totally appreciated, and presented the offer. Within five seconds he happily accepted my offer. He seemed extremely happy and somewhat shocked at what his collection was worth. He could not thank me enough for my time, patience, and expertise. He went on to say how much I put him at ease with the way I handled the transaction.

The exchange was agreed upon and the collection arrived in two large boxes the following Saturday. The cars were as nice, if not even better than they were in the pictures. It was the kind of surprise that I like in this hobby as compared to the opposite happening.

Where did he go? Short Round, it is now time to show the world the super stars of the San Luis Obispo, California original, one owner, Redline Era Hot Wheels collection. Oh, forget it Short Round, I got this. Ladies and Germs, I take great pleasure in presenting the "Champions" of the San Luis Obispo, CA collection. Please give them a standing ovation…..

1. **Python, LITE BLUE with White Interior**
2. **Custom Cougar, OLIVE with Black Roof and White Interior**
3. **Custom Camaro, BLUE with White Interior**
4. **Classic Cord, ROSE PINK**
5. **Snake II, WHITE ENAMEL**
6. **Mantis, HOT PINK**
7. **Custom Charger, GOLD**
8. **Porsche 917, MAGENTA with White Interior**
9. **Ferrari 312p, ORANGE**
10. **Custom Barracuda, RED with White Interior**
11. **Porsche 917 Blister Pack, HOT PINK with White Interior**
12. **Four Club Kit Magazines, two different variations**
13. **Classic '57-Bird, PURPLE with White Interior**
14. **Bye-Focal, AQUA**
15. **Noodlehead, RED**

There you have it, and once again, another unbelievable discovery out of the State of California and the result of a totally FREE marketing opportunity called "The Hustle." The power of the media at its finest.

Ok, fasten your seatbelts as we are embarking on a seventeen-hundred-mile trek directly north of the border to our great neighbors north of the border in British Columbia, CANADA where our next collection was unearthed. Right, right, I get it Short Round, there are no seat belts in our jeep either. Boy is it cold up there this time of year. Short Round, did you pack our winter gear? What do you mean we do not own any winter gear? Oh boy, bundle up, because it is going to be one cold ride. Brrrrrrrrrrr…

The BRITISH COLUMBIA Collection
Unearthed: 02.02.2021

Normally when my phone rings, the majority of the time I recognize the area code. In this case, I immediately did not and had to grab my reading glasses after rubbing my eyes. You know, what you do when you are either old or want to clear your vision. In this case, both scenarios apply. Ok, enough of the chuckles, let us move on. The call came in and I must say, I was surprised a bit. The gentleman on the other end of the line had the typical accent from those that reside north of the border. I played travel Ice Hockey as a kid and would travel to Toronto once a year to play multiple Canadian teams. I know the accent quite well as my teammates and I always tried to mimic it on the annual trips from New Jersey to Canada and back again, and while in Canada. Just something we did as crazy ice hockey players of the seventies. We would even catch ourselves, upon arriving back in the States, attempting to talk like our rivals to the north. It became a bit awkward around the dinner table when I would slip with an "AYY" or an "OUHT." My parents always gave me that confused look which was proceeded with the proverbial stink-eye, and that certainly was enough for me. I tended to lose the accent quite rapidly after just a couple of these encounters with the parents.

The owner of the collection and I hit it off almost immediately. We spoke at length in our initial phone call and remain in touch to this day. We are both former ice hockey players and religious NHL fans to this day. Not only did we have hockey and Redline Hot Wheels in common, but the more we talked, the more we both realized that we travelled similar paths in life during our youth.

The British Columbia, CANADA original one owner collection that contained cars that I have never found in the States after three decades of searching.

The provenance of the collection was the typical story that I had heard many times over the years. The cars were loved, played with, and then put away in storage never to be heard from again until only recently. This was certainly the case with this grouping of cars, race sets, and accessories. The gentleman said that he performed a search online and REDLINE ARCHEOLOGY popped right up in the number one spot. Kudos to my web designer Larry Siegel, CEO of Marketing Fusion (www.MarketingFusion.net) for promises kept. This demonstrates just how critically important it truly is to not only have a solid marketing plan in place but having the right individual(s) to implement it is just as important to your success in locating these elusive collections.

I asked the gentleman to send me some pictures via email as I did not want him or myself incurring any added costs by using our iPhones to text pictures. He agreed and sent me a ton of pictures of this dusty old collection that had not stretched its legs in over fifty years. The pictures did not disappoint in the least and I was rubbing my eyes again to make sure what I was seeing, was truly in front of me. One after another of some castings and colors I just have never found in any of the hundreds of collections I have scored over my career. Even as I write this, I find myself shaking my head thinking of these cars in question. And to boot, they all were in spectacular condition. Lucky me, eh? I try not to assume anything when appraising these collections and making an offer. Taking the emotion out of these deals is a necessity if you are going to be successful at it at any level. Always keep in the back of your mind that no one is ever obligated to sell you their collection of Redline Hot Wheels, no one. Leave your frustration at the front door is the best advice I can give you. It will end up serving you quite well.

Well, let us get back to the cars. One after another they just kept coming. One rare car after the other began appearing in my email. A rose Rocket-Bye-Baby, an aqua Sidekick, a salmon pink Swingin' Wing, lite green Strip Teaser, magenta Six Shooter, orange Rolls Royce Silver Shadow, green NO INJECTOR Bye-Focal, aqua with white interior Evil Weevil, blue with white interior Mercedes C-111, and a magenta (Berry) with white interior Sand Crab. There was a total of ninety-five Redlines from 1968 – 1971, five Sizzlers still in their plastic boxes, three Rrumblers, two Farbs, lots of loose accessories, and a few French-Canadian boxed accessories. The collection was nothing short of astounding to this hunter of Redlines.

The exceedingly difficult to find lite green Strip Teaser and magenta Six Shooter. Two pieces that have eluded me for my entire career until now.

I sharpened my pencil, cleaned my reading glasses, and got right to the appraisal on this first-timer from the Great North. Over the next few days, the owner of the collection and I must had spoken at least twice daily, not only about his breath-taking collection, but also about hockey, our favorite NHL teams, the sixties, and our parents. Fathers always seem to have had the greatest influence on us boys of the sixties and seventies when it came to the Redline Hot Wheels. My mother, however, was the exception to the rule, and was responsible for more, if not all my collection growing up. She worked at the JC Penney, Co. store in Audubon, New Jersey as a Personnel Specialist and her office was right past the Toy Department on the second floor. Yes, I said, "RIGHT PAST THE TOY DEPARTMENT!!!" Could the story have gotten any better back in 1968 for this little boy? I begged my father every Friday night to go with him to pick her up after work which was approximately nine o'clock at night. He usually agreed, but that was no guarantee that I was getting a "prize" of sorts. You know, a shiny new, cool, amazing, and incredible Redline Hot Wheel that I did not already possess. A kid can dream, can't he?

The toughest color for the Sidekick, aqua.

The appraisal was finally complete, so I picked up my phone and called my newfound Canadian friend to discuss his valuable collection. Like I stated earlier, I always carve out a block of time to discuss the collections 1) Most Valuable Car(s) 2) The Good News 3) The Bad News. Typically, the "Good News" refers to the collections overall value if high, and the "Bad News" refers to a collection's overall value if low or lower than expected. Thankfully, in this case, the news was mostly good. The offer was made and accepted immediately. Getting collections from Canada proved to be a slight adventure with Customs on both sides of the border, but all is well that ends well. This most certainly ended well for this Redline Archeologist, and in a big frozen way!

The elusive and much rarer No-Injector version of the Bye-Focal.

"Short Round, Short Round, where are you?" Oh well, let us keep the Redline wheels turning and pay homage to the "BEST OF THE GREAT NORTH" collection out of British Columbia, CANADA.

You all know the drill by now. Let us all stand up, stretch the old legs, and give a much-needed warm welcome to all our little frozen friends north of the border... The BEST of the BEST from the British Columbia CANADA original, one owner, Redline Era Hot Wheels Collection:

1. Sidekick, AQUA
2. Rocket-Bye-Baby, ROSE PINK
3. Swingin' Wing, SALMON PINK
4. Strip Teaser, LITE GREEN
5. Six Shooter, MAGENTA (Berry)
6. Mercedes C-111, BLUE with White Interior
7. Bye-Focal, GREEN with No Injectors
8. Evil Weevil, AQUA with White Interior
9. Sand Crab, MAGNETA (Berry) with White Interior
10. Rolls Royce Silver Shadow, ORANGE
11. Mighty Maverick, COPPER
12. Mutt Mobile, MAGEMTA
13. Short Order, YELLOW
14. Cockney Cab, OLIVE
15. Porsche 917, GREEN

I like to refer to this find out of Canada as history being made in my Redline career and universe. The first time I have unearthed an original Redline Era Hot Wheels collection north of the border. They say things happen in threes, so here is hoping that the next two collections are just around the icy, slippery, and snow-covered corner…

Ok everyone, the seat belt sign is back on, and the captain would like you all to take your assigned seat. Seat belts or no seat belts, we are heading directly south, fourteen hundred miles to be exact, to the town of Sacramento, California. I figured since we were already on the west coast we might as well stay a little bit longer… Right Short Round? Short Round, where did you go? Ow!!! Put the snowball down and get onboard as we head south back to the good ole U.S. of A….

The SACRAMENTO, CA Collection
Unearthed: 10.30.2020

The call came in a week before Halloween. Halloween has always been one of my favorite times of year. As a child, I was intrigued by all the old-time horror movies of the twenties, thirties, and forties. My Hollywood heroes of the day were Lon Chaney Sr. (Hunchback of Notre Dame, Phantom of the Opera), Bela Lugosi (Dracula), and Boris Karloff (Frankenstein). Lon Chaney Sr. was and remains my all-time favorite from the horror films he starred in. He was an amazing artist and actor and really scared the you know what out of this guy, but I loved every moment of it. His son, Lon Chaney Jr. (Wolfman) was no slouch himself. One Christmas, my parents gave me a subscription to Famous Monsters of Filmland monthly magazine that I always read cover to cover. I watched the mailbox every month and still remember how excited I was to receive each copy. I had the subscription for five years and saved every copy. Regretfully, I sold them all at a yard sale in the nineties to help pay down my college loans.

One thing that I am known for today where I reside is dressing up as Michael Myers and tormenting the neighborhood on Halloween. It goes over so well every year with all the parents and trick or treaters, that everyone seems to talk about it for weeks following Halloween. Sometimes my neighbors will wave to me as they are passing by yelling "Hi Michael." All in fun and the spirit of the day.

Oh yeah, the collection. I sometimes get side-tracked when the topic of Halloween comes up. Sorry, but I really get into the day. The phone rings and on the other end of the line is a gentleman from Sacramento, CA. You all know by now how I feel about collections from the Golden State. They are typically in pristine condition and sometimes un-played with. We talked for about fifteen minutes on our lives growing up in the sixties and seventies. We shared a few laughs and then moved onto the collection at hand.

The gentleman stated that he stumbled across my REDLINE ARCHEOLOGY YouTube Channel and found all the videos very entertaining and educational in nature. I always appreciate this type of feedback as I work awfully hard at producing videos that check both boxes. He went on to say that this prompted him to visit my website, RedlineArcheology.com, and try to learn more. He mentioned my BLOGS and information throughout the website as the driving force for him to go to his storage unit and look for his beloved Hot Wheels that he has not given much thought to for over fifty years.

One thing that I always make a point of doing is asking the owners their age right up front. A gentle way of doing this is to ask what year they were born. One thing my wife Deborah has taught me is that you never ask a woman her age or how much she weighs. Guys do not care, but I did learn the hard way, early on in life, that my wife was one hundred percent right. Word of advice: DO NOT EVER ASK A WOMAN HER AGE OR WEIGHT. The gentleman was a few years younger than I so I figured that the seventy threes and the Flying Colors would come into play in his collection due to his age. Flying Colors are a line of Hot Wheel cars that began production in 1974. I was right on the latter part but for some reason he skipped the year 1973 as far as Hot Wheels were concerned. I would have to safely assume that they just were not appealing to him as a kid. I think we all can understand this as Mattel had drastically cut costs that year due to a drop in sales, and inflation that was impacting the entire country. Enamel paint replaced the beautiful Spectraflame colors which was the main reason for the lack of excitement with kids and buyers of the day.

The Sacramento, CA original one owner collection with lots of Flying Colors.

We arrived at the time of the conversation when we started to discuss the details of the collection. He started to describe a lot of cars from my era such as the Snake & Mongoose, Mighty Maverick, and a bunch of cars from 1968 – 1972. The Flying Colors were next and there was a total of fourteen pieces from the era. Additionally, there were twenty-eight from the years 1968 - 1972. The most incredible part of this collection ended up being a couple of Flying Color pieces from 1975, and both were as factory fresh as imaginable. The yellow Mustang Stocker with blue and red stripes, and drumroll please…..the WHITE Mustang Stocker with blue and red stripes. Two incredible pieces that you could never upgrade in a million years.

The incredibly rare Mustang Stockers in yellow and white both with blue + red Stripes. White being rarer, especially in this blister pack condition example.

I asked for pictures from six different angles be sent to me either via email or text message. As a collector and appraiser, I request pictures from the top, bottom, front, back, and both sides of each car individually. Most sellers of these collections choose to text message as again, this is the easiest and most accessible way of providing high resolution pictures. My iPhone started to "ding" as the dozens of pictures started to flood my phone. Most, if not all the cars were in pristine un-played-with condition, and this was a very pleasant and welcomed surprise. I was sitting on the edge of my chair waiting for the pictures of both Mustang Stockers and boy they did not disappoint on any level. Looking back on the collection, they might have been the two cars in the absolute best overall condition. They both appeared flawless in the pictures but taking the cars in the natural sunlight is always the best judge of condition.

The alternate color and exceedingly rare white Mustang Stocker with blue and red stripes that every Redline collector would love to add to their collection, especially in this condition.

As a passionate Redline collector, I focus on the years 1968 – 1972 but do have an appreciation for the cars produced from 1973 and on. Flying Colors are cars that seem to appear in a significant amount of the collections I come across. Once I received all the pictures of every car contained within this amazing collection, I got right to work appraising every single one. Once my appraisal was completed, I reached out to the owner to have my required conversation of basically educating the individual on what the collection's overall retail value is at auction, the most valuable cars in the collection and why, and all other pertinent information, good or bad, that I feel is important, so the seller has all the facts. Once this aspect is thoroughly covered by me with the owner, I move on to making the offer. When expressing my offer, I also take the time to explain why it is lower than full retail value. I also discuss what is involved in online auctions if they choose to go that route. It is only fair to the individual so they can make the right decision for them with these valued and sentimental toy cars.

The rare Purple Mantis from 1970. A very cool concept car casting in a very desirable color.

The offer was presented, and I instructed him to take a day or so to think about it and then get back to me either way. Like buying a new car or home, which are always substantial purchases to most, as I stated earlier, I try to take the emotion out of these deals. Again, it is good common practice that has and continues to serve me well in the hobby. You cannot win them all and try not to expect to or you will be disappointed on a regular basis. He followed my advice and called me three days later to accept my generous offer.

The cars arrived the day before Halloween on October 30th, 2020. The collection was one that surprised me in a positive way. The cars were even better in hand. All the Flying Colors and Spectraflame era cars were in as nice of condition as you could possibly hope for.

A few examples of Flying Colors that were discovered in the collection. Super Chrome Large Charge (1975), Baja Bruiser (1974), and OLDS 442 Police Cruiser (1974).

So, there you have it. A collection that was thankfully dusted off after more than five decades in storage and ended up at the offices of REDLINE ARCHEOLOGY. I do not really have any offices, only my personal one that has Redlines surrounding me. It is the perfect, or should I say, blister pack freshest office in town. So here we go with all the blister pack fresh superstars out of the town of Sacramento, California... The "APPLAUSE" sign is lit!

1. **Mustang Stocker, WHITE with Blue + Red Stripes**
2. **Mustang Stocker, YELLOW with Blue + Red Stripes**
3. **1974 Police Cruiser**
4. **Mantis, PURPLE**
5. **Custom Charger, ORANGE**
6. **Funny Money**
7. **1975 Mighty Maverick**
8. **1975 Porsche 911, YELLOW**
9. **Custom AMX, ROSE PINK**
10. **Sand Crab, HOT PINK**

Short Round, Short Round, where did you go??? We have lots more collections to cover. Oh boy, I guess I am on my own now. Next up, we jump into the dirty, old Jeep and head just a few miles south to the lovely town of Lodi, California. Get ready, grab your favorite drink, favorite snack, and prepare yourself for the LODI, California original one owner Redline Era Hot Wheels collection. This one is a "doozie." Not that doozie, but the kind of doozie that is unique or one of a kind. Geesh, is that all you do is think about Hot Wheels all day? I have a confession to make, me too! Here we go.....

The Lodi, CA Collection
Unearthed: 03.07.2021

To say that this was an incredible collection with an incredible number of incredible cars in incredible condition, well, I think you get my point. I received an email through my contact page on my website from a gentleman in Lodi, California who had his collection of Hot Wheels from his childhood and was looking for a way to find out their true value. I asked him if he was considering selling the collection if the appraisal came back favorable in his eyes. He confirmed that he wanted to sell the collection but did not want to get taken advantage of due to his lack of knowledge of this toy car line.

I agreed to perform a full and thorough appraisal for him and his collection of old Hot Wheels and proceeded with attaining pictures. He decided to send me a Google Drive folder of all the pictures in detail. He did an amazing job taking the pictures and followed my directions to a "T" and then some. He sent more pictures than requested, but more is always better in a situation like this. One after another, the killer cars kept appearing as I was scrolling through all the pictures. I had not witnessed a collection this size bearing so much juicy, low hanging fruit in a long time. Yes, I have discovered collections with as many rare beauties as this one, but they were typically three times larger in size.

The breathtaking collection discovered in Lodi, California. Fifty-seven Redlines strong.

The green enamel Volkswagen appeared first, and I was like "Wow" this is the first time in my career that I ever landed one that appeared to be just pulled from Mattel's' factory line back in 1968. Next there appeared a magenta Carabo with a white interior followed by an aqua white interior Custom Camaro. I was floored and started thinking the show was over and all that was left were commons and cars that had been played with. I was proven wrong on so many levels with what was waiting in the wings preparing to show their beautiful Spectraflame paint to me.

The white interior Carabo surrounded by a bevy of beauties including a gold Classic 31 Ford Woody, red Short Order, and magenta Seasider. Eye candy for any passionate Redline collector.

They just kept coming, one after the other and with no end in sight. A purple with white interior Rolls Royce Silver Shadow appeared and I almost collapsed on the spot. Well, I am being a bit dramatic, but I did have to take another look to make sure what I was seeing was exactly that, a purple with white interior Rolls Royce Silver Shadow in what appeared to be blister pack fresh condition. Sometimes, nowadays with some of the smartphone cameras, blue can actually appear to be purple. I needed to make sure that this was truly one of the toughest colors in this casting. The Rolls Royce Silver Shadow in purple with a white interior is considered as being one of the toughest colors in this casting just behind the Hot Pink version. The seller confirmed that it was purple, and I could not have been more excited as this was the first time that I ever found a Rolls Royce Silver Shadow in any color other than grey enamel with a dark interior. I had finally dug up one of the two toughest colors in this casting. This just goes to show how truly rare a piece like this is, especially in the un-played with condition it appeared to be in.

The extremely rare purple with white interior Rolls Royce Silver Shadow flanked by a beautiful example of a magenta Classic Cord.

At this point the oxygen was not getting to my brain and I had to grab a small brown paper bag and…..well, no need to go any further with this. I was becoming increasingly curious on what my laptop screen would display next, and I was not left in the dark for long. There it was, right in front of my eyes, a blue Fleetside and a No Injector green Bye-Focal, both in head shaking condition. One after another, and it was like being on your favorite amusement park ride for hours. A purple with white interior King Kuda appeared, followed by a magenta Classic '36 Ford Coupe. I kept pinching myself thinking will this ever end. Beautiful car after beautiful car just kept appearing and showing me their stunningly gorgeous, little smiling faces. You know it is something to behold when a near perfect magenta Classic Cord is just another car in the collection. There were also four "Hot Strip Track Super Pak" sets still in their near mint boxes that were sealed on one end each. I had never seen this twenty-foot Hot Strip Super Track Pak before now. I did not even know they existed. The artwork on each box was like it just came out of print at Mattel back in 1969. Amazing pieces that finally appeared in a collection after all these years.

The All-Stars from the Lodi, CA collection. From left to right; rose Ford J-Car, green enamel Custom Volkswagen, blue Fleetside, aqua Custom Camaro, purple Rolls Royce Silver Shadow, magenta Carabo with white interior, magenta Classic 36 Ford Coupe, green No Injector Bye-Focal, and center: purple King Kuda with white interior.

So many beautiful cars and all in one place at the same time. Even all the other cars were mind-blowing. Yet just another day in the office with what was becoming a typical collection out of the Golden State. Clean, unplayed with, zero toning across the board, and obviously well-loved for over five decades. The State of California just keeps amazing me with every collection I unearth, time and time again. It truly is something to think about. So, without further ado, I would like to introduce the one and only, stupendous, amazing, phenomenal, incredible….. I am getting a bit carried away. The Lodi, California original one owner Redline Era Hot Wheels collection. Enjoy, I know I did…

1. Ford J-Car, ROSE
2. Custom Volkswagen, GREEN ENAMEL
3. Custom Fleetside, BLUE
4. Custom Camaro, AQUA with White Interior
5. Rolls Royce Silver Shadow, PURPLE
6. Carabo, MAGENTA with White Interior
7. Classic '36 Ford Coupe, MAGENTA
8. Bye-Focal, GREEN with No Injectors
9. King Kuda, PURPLE with White Interior
10. Mighty Maverick, YELLOW
11. Maserati Mistral, PURPLE with White Interior
12. Short Order, RED
13. Seasider, MAGENTA
14. Custom Eldorado, ORANGE with White Interior
15. Power Pad, HOT PINK
16. Classic Nomad, MAGENTA
17. Mercedes Benz 280sl, PURPLE
18. TNT Bird, BLUE with White Interior
19. Classic Cord, MAGENTA
20. Classic '31 Ford Woody, GOLD with White Interior

There they are, all the best of the best out of the collection from the small town of Lodi, California. Short Round start the engine and load up the Jeep. We are now heading due east to the Land of the Rolling Prairie and the wonderful state of Iowa. Our next stop on this glorious Redline tour is the small town of Red Oak, IA, with a population of just over five thousand residents. Do not let the size of this town fool you. What you are about to see is a discovery that only comes around once every ten years if you are lucky. Well, Short Round and I have a long drive ahead of us, so sit back and enjoy the scenery as we head to the official dig site in Red Oak, IA.

The Red Oak, IA Collection
Unearthed: 08.26.2020

In my world of diggin' up these wonderful original collections, it is always hard for me to rank them. If I were to rank all my hundreds of collections that I have unearthed over the last three decades, this collection would absolutely rank in the top five. You are about to see some cars that you probably have not only never laid eyes on before, but never knew existed in the Mattel Hot Wheels toy car line up. I personally will never forget this phenomenal grouping of cars. The number of cars in the collection will absolutely blow you away as a Redline enthusiast as well. So, let us get to it and explore the Red Oak, Iowa original one owner Redline Era Hot Wheels collection, shall we.

I initially received an email via my website from the original owner that did not have many details contained within. The only information that was expressed in the initial contact form from my website was that he read about me in the recent article from "The Hustle" online article which proved to be a total grand slam for me in the world of free advertising. When this happens, I always reply thanking the individual for the email and, I request pictures be sent to me of the collection at hand. As I have said, I always give the owner(s) a choice of either emailing or text messaging pictures to me. They typically text pictures to me as this is the easiest and quickest way of getting them out. In this case however, the pictures were sent to me via email. I only received one picture in the second email, but it was a doozie. Oh, come on… Again, not a Hot Wheels "Doozie", a real doozie. Geesh.

Initial Picture sent to me from the original owner of the Red Oak, IA Collection. One Hundred and Seventy- Five total Redlines

I was floored but I knew I had to quickly regain my composure and start looking at this massive collection up close and personal. I retrieved my professional jeweler's loupe magnifying head band and went to work. There is always a controlled method to my madness when looking at full group shots of collections. Due to the size of this collection, the only photo that I had to go by was not a close-up shot. The owner had to take the picture the way he did to capture each car in this incredibly large collection. I not only magnified the photo on my laptop, but I had to utilize my jeweler's loupe to further bring each car into focus enough to, at a minimum, identify the casting and color. Typically, I start in the back and work my way up to the front. First and foremost, I confirm that each car is a Redline and then count them all to reach a total. In this case there ended up being a total of one hundred and seventy-five Redline Hot Wheels.

If someone had filmed me going through this collection for the first time, they would have witnessed my jaw dropped, eyes wide open, my head shaking constantly, and words like "Are you kidding me", "What is that?" and "OMG" being uttered repeatedly. It was a collection like no other that I have seen, and I had to get to the bottom of this somewhat mind-boggling grouping of Redlines. There were a couple cars that I really could not make up my mind whether they were true Redlines or not, but we will get to this later. My next step was to contact the owner and request a time to discuss the collection. We agreed on a day and time and exchanged cell phone numbers. As the saying goes, "Days are long, but the Years Fly By." Well, in this case, the two days leading up to the initial phone call seemed to drag on like molasses running down a hill. The day finally arrived, and the owner called me at the exact agreed upon time. In my world, this is a real good sign. I take this as someone who is motivated to not only learn more about the collection and its value but are also extremely interested in selling. Just a gut instinct of mine that typically plays out.

The collection arrived safely to its' new home @ REDLINE ARCHEOLOGY.

I was not prepared for what I was about to hear from the owner of this phenomenal collection, but maybe I should have known what was coming after carefully looking at all the cars. I guess I was still in a bit of "Redline Shock" with all the interesting pieces contained within, that I have truly never seen before. When asked about the collection's provenance, the owner chuckled and told me a remarkably interesting story that started to put the pieces of this complicated Redline Hot Wheels puzzle together.

Back in the late sixties, the collection was assembled by the original owner with whom I was speaking with, but he had a lot of help from his cousin and Aunt and Uncle from, you guessed it, Southern California. He stated that each summer his relatives from southern California would visit him and his family in Iowa for a week each year. Every year, without missing a beat, his Aunt and Uncle would bring him a bag of loose and blister packed Hot Wheels as a gift. Keep in mind the owner was born the same year as me so now you realize that the years 1968 – 1972 were in total play. He had hit the lottery without even knowing it but wait, it gets better, so much better.

I started to dig deeper with my line of questioning, and it became apparent that his Aunt and Uncle both worked at Mattel, Inc. located in Hawthorne, CA at some capacity during this time. It was not clear what their titles were or if in fact they worked there full-time, part-time, or only for a short stint. The owner thought that they also had either access to the Factory Store through a friend that worked there or knew someone on the inside that would give them cars for their son, his cousin. Obviously, a lot of the cars made their way east to the western part of the State of Iowa and into the hands of the owner who took particularly good care of his childhood toys for the last fifty years. After a long conversation, we agreed that this collection certainly had a connection to a Mattel employee or employees back in the sixties, it just was never confirmed whether his Aunt and or Uncle spent a lot of time employed by Mattel during this period or they just had a connection to the factory or factory store. The owner safely assumed that either his Aunt or Uncle was employed at one time in the sixties by Mattel due to the number of cars they would bring during their summer visits to Iowa.

Some of the spectacular Spectraflame cars in the Red Oak, IA collection. US orange Custom Camaro and creamy pick Custom Volkswagen.

The collection revealed many amazing cars in extraordinary condition. Car after amazing car were lined up in all their glory just winking back at me. There was an orange and copper King Kuda with white interiors, four Custom Camaros in blue, two anti-freeze Custom Camaros, and one orange Custom Camaro with a white interior, four Custom Mustangs in (2) red and (2) gold, a blazing hot pink Cockney Cab, a flawless orange with white interior Mantis, three Ford J-Cars in lite blue, green, and purple, Four Custom Chargers in orange, two Custom Chargers in purple, and one Custom Charger in aqua. It never stopped raining beautiful and rare Redlines this wonderful summer day. This collection was so close to coming home that I could smell the orange track. It was so close yet, so far away from its home here at REDLINE ARCHEOLOGY. At least that is what was going through my Redline Hot

Wheel obsessed mind. Like I have stated earlier, you must take the emotion out of these deals if you are going to make the right decision as a buyer and collector. Think about it for a moment; how hard it was for me to listen to my own advice at this critical time. It was near impossible, and do not let anyone tell you any different. I had a really hard time attempting to take a step back from this once in a collector's lifetime collection of Redline Era Hot Wheels.

A slice of the collection showing a line-up of Mighty Mavericks, Classic 31 Ford Woody's, Custom Chargers, and Spoilers.

The owner of this amazing assembly of Redlines was very upfront and transparent with me regarding the fact that he was shopping the collection around to other collectors throughout the country. Competition in business and life is always good as far as I am concerned. It really keeps me on my toes and wanting to stay one step ahead. Competition keeps me sharp and thinking what I can do bigger and better. It is a good thing and do not let anyone tell you any different. I requested a lot of extra pictures of many of the cars, especially the ones I had never seen before and those I identified as more desirable and quite rare. He obliged and sent me dozens more of all the requested cars. Something happened while I was going through the myriad of extra pictures which was a first for me in this hobby. I stumbled across a car that appeared to be familiar yet visibly different in many ways. It was a red Classic '31 Ford Woody with a black crinkle roof. I know what you are thinking. Why would this common car be so different in this common color? Although I knew it was a Classic '31 Ford Woody as it was stamped on its base, but it looked like an old time "Huckster" that you would see in the cities in the early twentieth century. The roof behind the front seats had been removed and blended into the back bed area to appear like it was never separated. There was an oval shaped rear window professionally cut behind the driver and passenger seats as well that was obviously done with some sort of machine and machinist. Was it a custom or was it a Prototype? This was the question that immediately popped into my head.

The mind-boggling red Classic 31 Ford Woody in front of the entire collection out of Red Oak, IA.

Gathering a thorough and accurate history or provenance of a collection of this magnitude is vitally important, especially when faced with a few cars that rarely if ever appear in the hobby. I gathered all the pictures of the Red Woody and sent them out to my small network of long time and knowledgeable Redline collectors. The opinions were split right down the middle. Half of the collectors said it was just a custom created possibly by a Mattel employee from back in the day and the other half said that it was absolutely a prototype. It was also confirmed by a few collectors that a few similar Woody's have shown up in collections with ties to former Mattel employees, exactly like this Red one, but in different colors and overall condition. I always apply the twenty-four-hour rule in situations like this. In other words, I never jump to conclusions until all the facts and information are gathered from reliable sources before I form my own opinion or conclusion.

Is it a Prototype or Custom? You decide.

The oval shaped machined rear window in what may be a Prototype.

    Of all the stunning and rare cars that ended up in the collection, the red '31 Classic Ford Woody was the king. It did have a lot of stiff competition though with other beauties that were standing by and waiting to reveal themselves to me. Knowing that this collection was being shopped, kept me hyper aware so that I did not let it slip through my fingers without a fight. About a week went by from my initial call with the owner so I decided to send him a text to see where he was with the collection. He replied instantly and told me that he would like to talk to me over the weekend after he had a chance to talk to one of his family members so that he could update them on the other offers.

    At this point I had not made a formal offer as I was still gathering as much information on the red Classic '31 Ford Woody as well as a few other oddities in the collection. I just wanted to be as fair as possible to the seller and to myself so that I did not over or under pay for this breathtaking collection. The weekend came and my phone rang on Saturday morning. The gentleman was on the other end of the line and he proceeded to inform me that he had received two other sizable offers and asked if I was still interested in making an offer. I said resoundingly "YES" and proceeded to tell him what I was willing to pay. He was happy with the offer but advised me that he had to go back to the other two collectors, out of respect, to see if they wanted to counter. I am not a big fan of this type of back and forth as my initial offer is usually my best offer, but considering the collection in question, I was willing to play the game this one time.

Another oddity that appeared in the Red Oak, IA collection. A no-stripe hot pink Mighty Maverick.

The gentleman called me back a few hours later that day and said that only one of the two other collectors vying for this incredible collection was willing to up his initial offer. He had outbid me by five hundred dollars. I was not going to lose this collection over five hundred dollars, so I upped my bid, and in the long run, drove the other buyer out of the game. I had accomplished what I had set out to and that was to not let this thousand-pound Blue Fin Tuna off my hook. The buyer was extremely happy with my offer and what he ended up with for this collection of dollar toys that were basically given to him gratis over fifty years ago by his loving aunt and uncle. Both sides in this deal were exceedingly happy and I was preparing the check and USPS Priority envelope to mail. The collection took exactly one week to get to me as it arrived on the following Saturday, August 26th, 2020. I just sat there staring at the boxes that contained, what I considered, one of my greatest finds ever. It was a moment that I will not soon forget. I waited until the next day to unpack the cars when I knew the house would be quiet as my family was down at the Jersey Shore for the day. It was a special moment that required my full attention. I decided to invite my collector friend Bruce Pascal over to help me unpack the collection and next thing I knew, he was right there beside me enjoying this incredible moment.

Some of the astonishing cars in the Red Oak, IA collection.

It took me a couple hours to safely unpack and carefully organize this mind-boggling collection. Car after car in factory fresh condition just kept on coming. I was attempting to enjoy and take in every moment, but it was like trying to take a drink on a hot summer day out of an open fire hydrant. It was a Tsunami of Redlines that seemed to have no end in sight. To list all the cars in the collection would almost double the size of this book so I will spare my publisher and printer the headache.

Maestro, strike up the band and give me the biggest drumroll ever. Please stand, take off your hats, and pay your respects to this once in a Redline Collectors lifetime find. It gives me great pleasure and honor to introduce you all to the "Hall of Famers" from the one and only Red Oak, IA original one owner Redline Era Hot Wheels Collection:

1. **Classic 31 Ford Woody, RED – Prototype**
2. **Mighty Maverick, HOT PINK – NO STRIPE**
3. **King Kuda, ORANGE with White Interior**
4. **King Kuda, COPPER with White Interior**
5. **(2) Heavy Chevy, ORANGE with White Interior**
6. **(5) Custom Chargers, BLUE, ORANGE, (2) PURPLE, AQUA**
7. **(7) Classic Nomad, MAGENTA, ORANGE, PURPLE, RED, ROSE, LIME, HOT PINK**
8. **(4) Custom Camaro, (2) ANTIFREEZE, BLUE, ORANGE with White Interior**
9. **(3) Ford J-Car, LITE BLUE, PURPLE, GREEN**
10. **(4) Mantis, (2) MAGENTA, YELLOW, ORANGE with White Interior**
11. **(2) Custom Cougar, BLUE, ORANGE**
12. **Classic Cord, GREEN**
13. **(4) Custom Mustang, (2) RED, (2) GOLD**
14. **Cockney Cab, HOT PINK**
15. **Classic 57 Bird, ORANGE**

The room really heats up when talking about this amazing find out of Red Oak, Iowa. One that may not be rivalled soon, or maybe never. Every time I say something along these lines, a collection shows up that shakes the Redline world to its knees. Short Round, oh there you are. Warm up the jeep and let us get on the road to our next stop to the border town of El Paso, Texas. Only one thousand miles to the southeast. We should be there in no time, right Short Round? Short Round, Short Round, oh boy, where did he go??? Well, it is now time to visit the Great State of Texas or as we know, The Lone Star State. Short Round, there you are. Poor little guy was sleeping in the back of the jeep. Diggin' up Redlines is a tough and exhausting job, but someone's got to do it.

The El Paso, TX Collection
Unearthed: 12.10.2020

The Lone Star State has produced some amazing collections for me over the years, and this certainly was no exception. I was out to dinner with my wife and some friends when my phone rang. As a rule, I normally do not take my cell phone with me when going out to dinner. My wife brings hers just for emergencies. We have been doing this for years and it has worked out well for us without all the interruptions. For some reason on this occasion, I forgot to leave my phone at home. I excused myself from the table to answer the call. It had a California area code and came up as a call from "Sacramento, CA." It is nearly impossible for me to ignore a call from a California number I do not recognize. It is the passionate Redline Collector and Redline Archeologist in me that refuses to miss a potentially amazing collection of our favorite toy car.

On the other end of the line was a gentleman who was giggling a bit when I answered the phone. He apologized but stated that he was loving all my YOUTUBE Channel videos, and it took him back to an incredibly happy time in his life, and thus the chuckles. We spoke briefly as I did not want to be rude to my wife and friends as we had just sat down to enjoy a nice dinner out. I told him that I would call him back the next day and we agreed on a time. I always must ask what state they are living in, so I do not call them too early or too late. Afterall, not everyone lives on the east coast. He said that he was a couple hours behind me in El Paso, Texas so we planned our follow up call accordingly.

The next day I picked up my phone at the scheduled time and placed the call. He answered immediately, which, as I have stated earlier, is always a good sign when it comes to sellers. We chatted briefly about the time era in which we both grew up in and found out that we were literally born weeks apart in the same year of 1960. This is always welcomed information as I can safely assume that he has some of the Customs, Spoilers, and other desirable cars in his collection. He started to go through his large collection of Redlines and it was apparent that he began receiving Hot Wheels around the same time I did in 1968. The collection appeared to have spanned the same number of years as mine did from 1968 – 1972. The collection totaled sixty-six Redline Hot Wheels, a forty-eight-car flat case, a forty-eight-car stack case, a 1969 collectors' catalog, a 1970 collectors' catalog, and sixty-six collector buttons. It was a sizable yet typical collection to say the least.

As is common practice for me, I requested pictures be sent to me starting with overhead group shots and then moving onto specified cars from six angles individually. He obliged and I received the pictures later that day. To say that I was pleasantly surprised and mildly excited about this collection may be a bit understated, but WOW, I was not prepared for what I was about to see. One incredible car after another started to pop up on my screen.

My "Cheshire Cat Smile" grew with each passing picture. I was in Redline Heaven. My curiosity started to get the best of me like it always does with collections like this, so I called the gentlemen and began the process of gathering as much information related to the provenance of this remarkable collection as I possibly could.

The El Paso, TX Redline Collection that had its beginnings in Sacramento, CA.

He started to tell me as to where this spectacular collection had its origins. It was the State of California and in Sacramento to be exact. This is where he was born and raised until his teenage years when his parents decided to move the family to El Paso, TX where he has made his home ever since. So, there it was, once again, a collection out of California that just blew me away, AGAIN! The condition of each car was like they were each just ripped out of their blister pack and carefully placed in their assigned spot in a forty-eight-car case and left there for fifty plus years. California has struck again with bearing out another gem of a Redline Hot Wheels collection.

This is exactly why I always make sure to try and answer my phone when a California area code pops up. Not that I do not try to answer my phone all the time when I can, but a California number triggers that alarm just a little more in my mind when it comes to Redline Era Hot Wheels Collections.

I received all the requested extra pictures of the higher end and rarer cars, so I began the appraisal process. A few of the cars in the collection demanded a lot more attention because of their potential value. I did all my research and bounced a couple cars off a collector friend or two of mine to get their opinions. The appraisal was completed forty-eight hours later, and I proceeded to reach out to the owner to discuss the collection and make an offer that I was hoping he could not refuse. We discussed the collection in depth and were on the phone for at least an hour. With some sellers I seem to get side-tracked during these conversations and talk about all our experiences growing up in the sixties. We always seem to have walked sort of the same paths in life during this time and it always stirs up good stories and great memories.

We got to the offer and he was thrilled with what I was willing to pay for his precious collection and he accepted immediately. The rest as they say is Lone Star State Redline history. The collection arrived at my house on Thursday, December 10, 2020. A beautiful collection that will be enjoyed for years by myself and some other lucky Redline collectors.

The incredibly rare and blister pack fresh Hong Kong Custom Barracuda with a white interior and an amazing US Custom Charger.

So, let us get right to it. Here are all the "Best of the Best" from the spectacular Spectraflame Redline Hot Wheels Collection out of, well, Sacramento, CA and El Paso, TX:

1. *Custom Barracuda, ORANGE with White Interior*
2. *Custom Charger, ORANGE*
3. *Custom Camaro, GREEN*
4. *Custom Corvette, GREEN*
5. *Deora, RED*
6. *Mod Quad, MAGENTA*
7. *Mighty Maverick, APPLE GREEN*
8. *Porsche 917, APPLE GREEN*
9. *Ford J-Car, WHITE ENAMEL*
10. *Rocket Bye Baby, BLUE*
11. *Custom Continental MK IV, ROSE*
12. *Beach Bomb, AQUA with White Interior*
13. *Custom Volkswagen, GREEN with White Interior*
14. *Classic 57 Bird, ROSE*
15. *Custom Barracuda, GREEN*

The very cool apple green Mighty Maverick and green Custom Corvette with a white interior.

Chalk another one up for the State of California that ended up in the Lone Star State and town of El Paso, Texas. Yet just another example of a stunning collection born out of a dry climate. Certainly, there is something to be said about these collections that either originate or end up in a dry year-round desert like climate.

Ok Short Round, it is that time again. We need to get back on the dusty road to our next dig site. Time to dust off the hat, pack the bags, and get on the road. This time we head to the "Heart of it All" and the "Birthplace of Aviation", the wonderful State of OHIO. Make sure the tank is full Short Round, we have seventeen hundred miles to cover. Introducing the Circlesville, OHIO original, one owner Redline Era Hot Wheels Collection....

The Circlesville, OH Collection
Unearthed: 03.11.2021

Historically, Ohio has been a state that has not produced a lot of collections for me over the years, but, when it does, it never disappoints. This collection that came in on March 11th, 2021 was one that will not soon be forgotten by this Redline Archeologist. The initial contact was made via email through my website. I got the ball rolling immediately requesting group shots of the entire collection. In the initial email, the owner provided me with some information on the size of the collection being a total of sixty-nine cars with some collector's buttons. I was stoked and could not wait to see this original collection out of a state that is normally quiet in the Redline Archeology world.

The gentleman sent me a dozen or so pictures of mainly overhead large and small group shots. Immediately a couple of Black Roof Spoilers jumped out at me and this got the adrenaline flowing. Once I reviewed these initial pictures, I reached out to the owner and requested a phone call. We went ahead and scheduled the call for the following day so that I could get to know the owner better and learn more about his, what was shaping up to be, amazing collection. I always make sure I take a step back during these scheduled calls and take some time to educate the owner(s) on what makes his or her collection initially either incredibly value, disappointingly having little value, or somewhere in between. Most of the time this is greatly appreciated by the owner(s) of these hard-to-find collections.

Once I went through the process of discussing the collection and its potential value, I asked about the collection's provenance as I always do. Again, the owner was born the same year as I was in 1960 and we shared a lot of similar stories. Like I have said before, I find that people in my generation that grew up in similar suburban post World War II towns, travelled down similar roads in life in the sixties and seventies. It is a common theme I have found, over the last thirty years, with all the interesting people I meet along the way. He was the son of a World War II veteran like myself, but his father was stationed in Europe whereas my father was stationed in the

South Pacific, the Philippines to be exact. We talked for what seemed like an hour about our fathers and shared our personal stories and experiences of growing up as "Baby Boomers" in the sixties and seventies. We could have talked for hours but life was getting in the way, so we moved on to the history or provenance of the collection.

One of the few Redline Era collections unearthed by me in the last thirty years in the State of OHIO.

The gentleman went on to tell me a similar story about his collection that I have heard many times before, but it was still interesting for me to hear. He said that he received his first Hot Wheel at Christmas in 1968 and it was a magenta Silhouette. He also stated that he received more cars that day from relatives but could not recollect which exact ones. His birthday the following year was all Hot Wheels which made him extremely happy as they were his favorite toy . He said for the next four years, up until 1972, all he ever asked for was Hot Wheels and the race sets that went with them. He did have a Funny Money in his collection, just like I did, but that was where his collecting ceased, and his interest switched to girls. Like I said, we had a remarkably similar story.

The "Heroes" of the Circlesville, OHIO Collection.

The remainder of the pictures that I had requested during our call were sent and received so I proceeded with the appraisal process of this collection that was shaping up to be a historic find out of a state that normally is very stingy with its Redline Hot Wheels collections. The collection yielded a lot of incredibly clean, desirable, and rare cars. Over ninety percent of the cars contained within were in factory fresh condition and appeared to have never been taken out of their case and never run down the famous orange track. Shaking my head as I appraised every car, I wrapped up the valuation and placed a call to the owner to discuss the collection and make my more than fair offer.

The two MVPs of the Circlesville, OHIO Collection. Black roof white interior OLIVE Boss Hoss + black roof white interior King Kuda.

The three Runner-Ups, the lite blue Custom VW, creamy pink Custom VW, + apple green Custom VW all with white interiors.

I presented all the information regarding the collection and more specifically what the most valuable cars were and why. Owners always get excited when this kind of information is offered to them, as I can assume, they start seeing more and more dollar signs. Do not get me wrong, this is an incredibly positive and generous part of the appraisal process. You need to do this every time with every collection you stumble across if you want to be successful at closing the deal. I vocalized my offer and told him to take a day or so to think about it before deciding on which way to go. He called me back three days later to graciously accept my offer. He went on to tell me that my offer was significantly higher than all the others he received. He also said that he felt extremely comfortable with me and thanked me for my patience and all the interesting information I provided him regarding his wonderful collection of Redline Hot Wheels.

The collection arrived on Thursday March 11th, 2021 and I could not wait to open it and unwrap every little gem that was now lying right in front of me. The cars did not disappoint on any level. In fact, I was surprised how clean most of the cars ended up being. The pictures sometimes do not tell the whole story, but this story had a much happier ending than was expected. A GREAT FIND from a place where Redline Collections are somewhat scarce. Please give a resounding round of applause for all the gems out of the Circlesville, OHIO original, one owner Redline Era Hot Wheels Collection. Enjoy:

1. *King Kuda, BLUE with Black Roof and White Interior*
2. *Boss Hoss, OLIVE with Black Roof and White Interior*
3. *Custom Camaro, GREEN with White Interior*
4. *Custom Charger, APPLE GREEN*
5. *Porsche 917, APPLE GREEN*
6. *Custom Volkswagen, LITE BLUE with White Interior*
7. *Custom Volkswagen, CREAMY PINK with White Interior*
8. *Custom Volkswagen, APPLE GREEN with White Interior*
9. *Sugar Caddy, LITE GREEN*
10. *Beach Bomb, BLUE with White Interior*
11. *Custom AMX, APPLE GREEN*
12. *AMX II, RED*
13. *Custom Barracuda, PURPLE with Purple Interior*
14. *Custom Eldorado, RED*
15. *Mighty Maverick, RED*

Well, there it is, the Circlesville, OHIO collection. One unique find out of a state that does not easily let go of its' Redlines. I just want to take a moment and sincerely thank the State of OHIO for this wonderful gift to the Redline Collector world. Very much appreciated.

Short Round, nice to see that the jeep is packed, fueled up, and ready for our next adventure to the state of, well, wait a minute, forget about the car, we need our prop plane. We are headed to one of the Aloha Islands in the beautiful state of Hawaii. Leave the keys to the jeep behind Short Round, we are off to the local airport to grab our puddle jumper and onto the South Pacific to the little town of Kamuela, Hawaii. Prepare yourselves for this one folks. Introducing the Kamuela, Hawaii original, one owner Redline Era Hot Wheels Collection.

The Kamuela, HI Collection
Unearthed: 06.24.2019

The moment the number popped up on my phone with an area code of "808" I knew that something that has never happened to me before was about to occur. It was a call from the big island of Hawaii in a little town called Kamuela, formerly known as Waimea. Nicknamed "Cowboy Country" by some locals, Kamuela is home to Parker Ranch which is considered one of the oldest cattle ranches in the United States. With a population of approximately nine thousand residents, the town was similar in size to where I grew up in Stratford, New Jersey. Well, I know it is very tough to compare the two towns geographically and culturally, but I can assure you I had just as much if not more fun and excitement growing up in Stratford, New Jersey as I would have had anywhere else, including the beautiful state of Hawaii. So proud of my hometown. Can you tell? Was it something I said?

I answered the phone with my canned greeting "REDLINE ARCHEOLOGY, this is Bob", as I always do when I do not recognize a number from outside my area. On the other end of the phone was a nice guy who immediately introduced himself, right off the bat, as a lawyer. I thought to myself, what in the world would a lawyer from Hawaii possibly want with this Redline Hot Wheels collector. To my surprise, he had his original collection of Hot Wheels that he wanted to find out the value of and was considering selling it if the price was right. I assured him that he had dialed the right number and found the right guy to properly appraise his cars and race sets and make him a more than reasonable and fair offer. He seemed a bit apprehensive, but following a brief conversation, he agreed to send me an overhead group shot of his collection. The collection ended up bearing sixty-two Redlines from the years 1968 – 1971, two Johnny Lightnings, one Matchbox Carrying Case, one twelve car Rally Carrying Case, and one twenty-four car Flat Collectors Carrying Case. It was a nice collection, and I was excited to see if I could bring this one home across the large pond called the Pacific Ocean to the offices at REDLINE ARCHEOLOGY. I went ahead and reviewed the overhead group shot and requested additional pictures of approximately twelve more cars. The gentleman obliged and we were off to the pineapple races.

The first original Redline Collection to be unearthed in the Aloha State of Hawaii.

      The appraisal was completed, and I reached out to the owner to discuss all the details as I routinely do. He was more than happy with the outcome of the appraisal and was anxious to hear what I was going to offer. I verbalized my offer with the instructions to take a few days to think it over. He took about a week which is when my initial offers typically expire. My offers are good for seven days as I know this hobby and values of the cars can change on a dime and sometimes not for the better. The deadline of seven days is always expressed verbally and in writing when I make the initial offer on a collection, any collection.

The stunningly beautiful and desirable ice blue Custom Barracuda with a white interior.

The seventh day was upon us when that funny looking number popped up again on my phone and I knew immediately who was on the other end. The gentleman agreed to accept my offer but there were stipulations attached before the deal could be finalized. Being a lawyer, and us not knowing each other, there was some skepticism flowing around how funds were going to be guaranteed and sent at the same time I was getting assurances that the entire collection would be delivered to me safely and securely as well.

One of the tougher pieces to find in any Redline collection is this near mint example of a Sky Show Fleetside in purple, my favorite color!

Well, there is always a first time for everything as they say, and this was one of those times. I was asked to execute a sales agreement and have it notarized before closing the deal. I had zero problem with this as it protected us both. I fully understand the hesitancy from owners of these valuable entities when shipping cars cross country to a virtually complete stranger. I totally get it. I agreed to the terms of the deal and the paperwork was sent over to me the following day. I went to my local bank and executed the document and had it officially notarized. The document was scanned and sent right over to the gentleman as well as me dropping the original in the mail to him via USPS Priority Mail. It arrived in a few days, and the deal was done as the cars arrived shortly thereafter. All is well that ends well, I guess.

The cars surprised me in a good way as they appeared to have some minor play wear on just a few, yet most were as nice as they come. I thought for sure that there may have been some issues related to living near salt water for all those years, but that did not factor into this collection at all, and I was pleasantly surprised. It was not an unusual collection, but more of a typical sized collection that I find fairly frequently. The great part about it was the cars that it produced. Here are the "Champions" of the original one owner Redline Era Hot Wheels Collection out of, you guessed it, Kamuela, Hawaii:

1. *Custom Barracda, ICE BLUE with a White Interior*
2. *Sky Show Fleetside, PURPLE with Original Ramp and Stickers*
3. *Custom Mustang, ANTIFREEZE*
4. *Custom Mustang, RED with White Interior*
5. *Custom Camaro, GREEN*
6. *Custom Charger, PURPLE*
7. *Custom Continental MK IV, PURPLE*
8. *Classic 31 Ford Woody, ICE BLUE with White Interior*
9. *Beach Bomb, RED*
10. *Custom Corvette, RED with White Interior*
11. *Custom Corvette, GREEN*
12. *King Kuda, LITE BLUE*
13. *Classic Nomad, ORANGE*
14. *Custom Eldorado, ROSE PINK*
15. *Classic 36 Ford Coupe, GOLD*

Well, it is time to take one more dip in the beautiful turquoise waters off the coast of the big island of Hawaii and get back to the airport as we venture off on a long four-thousand-mile flight to the "Show Me" state of Missouri, and to the friendly town of Wildwood. Population: Thirty-Five thousand and counting. Short Round, please prepare for take-off and grab me a blanket and pillow. Hello, Short Round, Short Round. Poor little guy is fast asleep from this long journey. Oh well, I will get it myself.

It gives me great pleasure to introduce the original, one owner Redline Era Hot Wheels Collection from Wildwood, Missouri. Maestro, the usual please….

The Wildwood, MO Collection
Unearthed: 11.20.2020

"Spring will soon be gone (Wildwood Days), Summer's comin' on (Wildwood Days), And I'm-a dreamin' of (Wildwood Days), Lotsa summer love (bup-a-dup-a-dup-a-up), And all I think about (Wildwood Days), After school is out (Wildwood Days), Headin' down the shore (Wildwood Days), To have a ball once more…. Come on everyone, Whoa whoa whoa whoa those Wildwood days, wild wild Wildwood days, Oh baby…. Well, I guess you had to grow up in South Jersey to understand, but I just could not resist. I can guarantee there are some of you right now that will have that wonderful song by Bobby Rydell stuck in your head for at least a day or two now. Can you guess where this next amazing find originated? WRONG! Wildwood, Missouri to be exact. Who knew that there was another Wildwood other than our beloved little coastal town, with an amazing boardwalk, gigantic beaches, and yes, lots of carnival rides and games? Wildwood, New Jersey to be exact.

The call came in on a Tuesday in November 2020 right before Thanksgiving. The Fall of 2020 proved to be one of the most epic times of my career for scoring incredible, original, one owner Redline Hot Wheels collections. I credit "The Hustle" online article for a significant amount of this success. This one did not disappoint at any level. Collections were pouring in, day after day, week after week, and I was in the middle of what I like to call a "Redline Tsunami." The owner on the other end of the phone was a very polite and pleasant man who could not thank me enough for not only taking his call but for also educating him on my process of the appraisal. I gave him the two options of getting pictures of his collection to me and he chose to text message me a slew of them. The collection totaled seventy cars with their collector buttons, a seventy-two-car Stack Case, a twenty-four-car Rally Wheel Case, and two Collector Catalogs. What made this original collection special to me as a fervent Redline Hot Wheels enthusiast was the fact that not only were there some rare cars contained within, but the overall condition of the cars was pretty much stellar. Again, yet another sizeable collection with cars that looked like they were just painted at the Mattel factory in Hawthorne, California in the late sixties.

The Wildwood, MO entire seventy car collection in all its beauty.

The appraisal was complete, and the offer was put out there in cyberspace. The gentleman was extremely happy with my offer and accepted it immediately. The collection arrived on my front doorstep on the morning of Saturday November 20, 2020. It was one of the easiest transactions in my career. Some people are just trusting souls from start to finish.

I normally attend the local Cars and Coffee event every Saturday but this day I stayed home instead anticipating the arrival of this potentially extraordinary original collection. I started to unpack the cars and one after another looked better in my hands than did in the pictures. I was shocked and incredibly happy at the same time. Sometimes it can go the other way and you end up questioning why you paid what you did, but certainly not this time. Just like any business venture, there are risks involved almost every step of the way. In the end, this collection was everything I thought it was and so much more. Some beautiful and rarely seen cars were in this grouping and are now part of my personal collection.

The rare and ridiculously hard to find purple Nitty Gritty Kitty with a white interior.

The very desirable rose pink Beach Bomb in all its glory.

Oh baby, every day's a holiday and every night is a Saturday night, Oh those Wildwood days…. Introducing all the Best of the Beach (or "Shore" as we say in Jersey). Well, gimme a break, I will always be a Jersey Boy at heart and am still sticking with it. So here they are. The top sun-drenched stars from, ok ok, Wildwood, Missouri…. Geesh!

1. *Nitty Gritty Kitty, PURPLE with White Interior*
2. *Beach Bomb, ROSE PINK*
3. *Classic Cord, RED*
4. *Custom Barracuda, PURPLE*
5. *Custom Mustang, GOLD, Open Hood Scoop*
6. *Custom AMX, ORANGE*
7. *Short Order, RED*
8. *Custom Corvette, AQUA with White Interior*
9. *Custom Cougar, ORANGE*
10. *Custom Charger, BLUE*

Whoa whoa whoa, so, there it is, the Wildwood, Missouri original one owner Redline Era Hot Wheels Collection. Bobby Rydell would certainly be proud.

Short Round, point the compass directly east to my home state of New Jersey. We are headed to the southern part of the state where our next collection is patiently waiting for us. Introducing the Southern New Jersey collection…. No drumroll yet Maestro. I will certainly let you know when the next one is needed. Soon my friend, real soon.

The SOUTHERN NEW JERSEY Collection
Unearthed: 11.27.2020

Approximately thirty years ago when I first got started on my desire to dig up the original collections based on the first ten years of production of Hot Wheels, exploring the local market was the only option at the time. Trying to locate a collection outside of the circulation area of the two newspapers that I advertised in was not even a thought. The Philadelphia Inquirer and the Courier-Post were the only two publications that I would advertise in the "Wanted to Buy" section of the Classified Ads. Both papers covered the immediate Philadelphia and Southern New Jersey regions. My grass roots approach only took me as far as I was willing to drive, which was about an hour or two in any direction. It was just what the times dictated to me as a Redline Archeologist, and I was fine with it. I really did not know any better. Obviously, my reach only allowed a limited and targeted area to search out and locate the low hanging fruit per se. It proved to be enough to keep me busy, and I was certainly pleased with all the results.

Nowadays the tables have turned, and the scenario has completely reversed itself. Finding local collections is now a rarity and one that hardly ever surfaces. This time was different though, and a collection was offered to me which I credit to my consistent networking efforts at a local Hot Wheels Club and its membership. Do not get me wrong, I enjoy attending the club meetings from time to time, but you must never let any opportunity slip through your hands if you are to continue to be successful at this. This was the perfect example of always having your business card handy and getting the word out that you are "The Guy" to sell your original Redline Era Hot Wheels to.

A rare local collection in South Jersey that made its way home to Redline Archeology.

I make it a common practice to never buy from collectors, and I have my reasons for not doing so. This time the gentleman was not only a collector, but I also consider him a friend who I met through the local Hot Wheels Club. The collection he offered me was quite unique as well. The story goes that he purchased the collection from a retired police officer friend of his about three years prior. He never thought that he would ever sell the entire collection, so he kept it basically all together except for a few pieces. He decided to sell the collection to replenish some much-needed funds for the hobby, and he asked me if I was interested. Since I knew the collector well, trusted him, and considered him a friend, I told him that I was interested. I made the rare exception due to the fact that this was an original, one owner collection that was basically still in its original state.

We met at one of the monthly club meetings in South Jersey where he had laid out the collection on a couple of tables so I could see them firsthand and take some pictures to perform a thorough appraisal. I went home and put my pencil to the paper and got right on the appraisal of this large and spectacular collection with roots right in my backyard. I called my buddy the next day and went over the entire collection and made him the offer. I told him to take as much time as he needed as I felt there was a bit of hesitancy on his end to let this collection go. He eventually called me back about five days later and graciously accepted my generous offer. Both parties were extremely happy, and the rest is Jersey history.

One of the rarest and most sought-after castings in the Redline Hot Wheels world, the LITE BLUE Olds 442.

The collection was not stingy with rare and blister pack fresh examples of castings you do not normally see in these types of collections. Finding an OLDS 442 in any color or condition is a very odd and rare occurrence, but this collection produced one of the nicest condition LITE BLUE examples I have ever witnessed. Controversy has always surrounded the LITE BLUE OLDS 442 with two schools of thought attached to it as whether it was a true production color produced for the casting. The argument stems to as to whether Mattel purposely intended to produce an OLDS 442 in LITE BLUE or if in fact, the darker BLUE version was just sprayed lighter at times which produced what we identify as LITE BLUE in the hobby. Some collectors believe that the LITE BLUE version is a faded result of the regular production BLUE. I personally have a hard time with this philosophy as this version normally has very even paint that does not appear faded at all, but this is my professional opinion. Take it for what it is worth. The argument may never be settled unless some documentation or memo is produced or brought forward from this period at Mattel that lists all the authorized colors of this rare casting. We may never know, but one thing I do know is that the car found in this collection was a stunning LITE BLUE OLDS 442.

The rare white interior variation of the RED Indy Eagle discovered in the Southern NJ Collection.

The SALMON PINK Noodlehead.

This local collection close to my home was a genuinely nice and welcomed surprise in the Fall of 2020. The collection totaled eighty-cars, a twelve-car Rally Case, a twenty-four car Super Rally Case, two twenty-four Stack Cases, and one forty-eight car Stack Case. A spectacular grouping of Redlines all in one beautiful place. Here we go with the Southern Jersey STARS....

1. *OLDS 442, LITE BLUE*
2. *Indy Eagle, RED with White Interior*
3. *Noodlehead, SALMON PINK*
4. *Boss Hoss, AQUA with Black Roof*
5. *Ford Mk IV, LITE BLUE*
6. *Custom Mustang, GOLD*
7. *Bye-Focal, MAGENTA*
8. *Classic Nomad, HOT PINK*
9. *Custom Camaro, GREEN*
10. *Custom Eldorado, GOLD with White Interior*

Well, it is that time again. Time to get on the road or in the air to get to our next destination. Short Round, where are we headed this time? Short Round, where are you going on your bike? What do you mean it is only fifteen minutes down the road? Oh my, yet another local find within biking distance obviously. Short Round, let me get on the handlebars and you can pedal us both there. We are now destined for a quaint little town called Blue Anchor, New Jersey, located smack dab in the middle of the Pine Barrens and home to the infamous Jersey

Devil. We better get home before dark Short Round, just sayin'. It gives me great pleasure to introduce the BLUE ANCHOR, New Jersey original one owner REDLINE Era Hot Wheels Collection. Ripped from the claws of the Jersey Devil. Not really, just sounds good!

The BLUE ANCHOR, NJ Collection
Unearthed: 05.24.2019

My phone rang and up popped a local area code. Normally, this is a robo-call offering healthcare or extending one of my cars' warranty. I normally always answer my phone when it rings but am somewhat hesitant with local calls where I do not recognize the number. Nine times out of ten, it's just a solicitation type of call. I decided to pick up my phone, fully expecting to hear a recorded voice telling me all about healthcare coverage, which fortunately I do not need. This time was different, quite different. On the other end of the phone was a gentleman who sounded to be older, like me, asking whether I buy old Hot Wheels and their race sets. I, of course answered in the affirmative, so I ventured into my normal line of questioning. I asked him to open one of the cases and pull out a few cars, turn them upside down, and tell me their respective names. It took a couple of minutes, but the gentleman complied, and we were off to the Snake and Mongoose races. He named a Heavyweight and a few Customs. He said that the Customs were his favorite as a child. The conversation continued and he started to describe everything from a complete Sky Show Set in the box, to Chop Cycles, Club Kits, Rrumblers, and many other things related to the Redline Era line of Hot Wheels. I was literally blown away with everything he was mentioning that was part of this massive collection. I told the gentleman that he must have had incredibly generous parents with all the stuff he had in his possession from his childhood. He chuckled, agreed, and we decided to move onto the part of the conversation of when we could meet so that I could see the collection firsthand. Afterall, he was local to where I called home. He told me to "come on down" anytime that was convenient for me as he was off all week on vacation from his job at one of the Atlantic City casinos. I dropped everything and told him I would be there shortly as it was only ten miles from my new home. I had just moved back to New Jersey from living in San Diego, California for five years. Another exciting twist to this collection was that I was hosting an "East Coast Redliners" meeting at my house the next day and was expecting over fifty collectors from the surrounding states. I got to thinking that this would be something to display at the meeting if I were fortunate enough to make a deal for the entire collection.

It was Friday May 24th, 2019 to be exact. I was preparing the house for the wave of Redline Enthusiasts that were arriving the next day at approximately 11am. Redline collectors are never late and ALWAYS early if you know what I mean. So, I attained the gentleman's address and was off. I took a short cut and drove through the Pine Barrens to get to this house, avoiding all the major highways and traffic. Afterall, this was my home territory and stomping ground for many years, and I know the area like the back of my hand. I arrived right on time and drove up his long, dirt driveway. I saw him sitting on his large southern-type front porch and he greeted me with a kind hello and a cold frosty can of beer. I chuckled and thanked him, but beer is not on my radar, ever. No offense, but I prefer the red grapes to brewer's yeast and hops. He invited me into his home and directed me to his family room where the collection was literally covering most of the floor.

The breathtaking local Blue Anchor, NJ one owner collection.

I was so happy that a local collection like this was right in front of me, and I had the opportunity to see the collection in hand to appraise instead of having to depend only on pictures. It took me back to the good ole days in the nineties when I first got started on my journey of diggin' up Redline Era Hot Wheels collections. The collection was, in one word, breathtaking. I had a hard time initially wrapping my mind and eyes around the massive collection of cars, club kits, sticker sheets, cases, race sets, and lots of accessories that were just begging me to take them home. I was more than willing to oblige but you just never know what a seller's expectations are and how sincere they are about selling their beloved childhood memories. Like I said earlier, I try to always take the emotion out of these deals, but sometimes it is nearly impossible, especially in a situation like this one.

Twelve car tray sample of the seventy-one-car collection.

Car after car were just sitting there in their designated compartments in each respective tray and case in factory fresh condition. One after another, and then the Chop Cycles showed themselves, six in all. The elusive Zopter and Sky Show sticker sheets that looked like they were just pulled from their brand-new boxes off the store shelves. Multiple Club Kits with their original mailing envelopes. It just kept going and going and it felt like there was no end in sight. This was truly a Redliner's dream. I knew I had my work cut out for me, so I got right to it. I pulled out my notebook and starting with the first Stack Case and moved on to the Super Rally Case. Cars were stuffed in both, so I gingerly pulled each one out, one at a time, over the next two hours. In the end, there were seventy-one of the most beautiful Redlines I had ever witnessed. All the accessories were remarkable. Even all the collector buttons were there with each car, and the most sought after one smiling back at me, the OLDS 442 plastic edition. My heart was beating faster as time went on and I was having a hard time not showing my utter excitement.

Two of the most sought after and rare buttons in the hobby. The plastic Classic Cord and OLDS 442.

The time had come, and a few beers later, not for me, I was ready to discuss the collection with the owner. As always, I talked about his most valuable cars, and there were plenty. I worked my way down to the commons and lesser valued cars and then moved onto the rarely seen Chop Cycles and all the other accessories that had significant value in my opinion. The appraisal took me a bit longer than usual as I had to do some added research on some of the unique items that were directly in front of me. We chatted a bit about growing up in South Jersey and had a few laughs along the way. We shared similar experiences and it was discovered that we had some mutual acquaintances as well. It is a small world we do live in at times, and this was no exception. I presented my generous offer and the gentlemen looked at me for a minute and then focused his attention on his favorite cars, the customs. He got off onto a bit of a tangent, but I just sat there and listened patiently while he travelled down memory lane one last time with his cherished Hot Wheels of yesteryear. I have witnessed this many times over the years. Owners just want to spend a little more time before they let go. This was certainly the case with this owner and collection. I understood completely and let him have his final moments with his childhood memories. We negotiated a bit and finally landed on a number that we were both happy and comfortable with. One final celebratory beer was opened, and the deal was done. Fireworks went off in my head and the skies opened and the sun was shining so brightly. Yes, this is how it feels when scoring a collection of this magnitude and a feeling that has never diminished over time. One that I hope every Redline Hot Wheels Collector gets to experience at least once in their careers.

Some of the rare sticker sheets and items found in the Blue Anchor, NJ collection.

Another local collection in the books and so refreshing to see in person to evaluate. Meeting the individual owners, face to face, is also an interesting aspect of the entire experience and one that I always enjoy and cherish. Maestro, this one most definitely deserves a lead in with a drumroll. It gives me the distinct honor and privilege to introduce to you, the Local Champions out of Blue Anchor, New Jersey... Enjoy!

1. *Classic Cord, BLUE*
2. *Sugar Caddy, YELLOW*
3. *Custom Camaro, BLUE*
4. *Beach Bomb, BLUE with White Interior*
5. *Tow Truck, OLIVE with White Interior*
6. *Grasshopper, HOT PINK*
7. *Carabo, BLUE*
8. *Deora, PURPLE*

9. *Jet Threat*, YELLOW
10. *Ferrari 312p*, HOT PINK
11. *Tri-Baby*, SALMON PINK
12. *Bye-Focal*, MAGENTA
13. *Cockney Cab*, RED
14. *Bugeye*, BLUE
15. *Mutt Mobile*, BLUE
16. *OLD 442*, MAGENTA
17. *Classic '57-Bird*, YELLOW
18. *Snake II*, WHITE ENAMEL
19. *AMX II*, APPLE GREEN
20. *Mighty Maverick*, MAGENTA

Short Round, put some air in the bike's tires and let us get on the road. I feel a certain set of eyes on us, and we need to get back before the sun goes down. We are, after all, in the Jersey Pine Barrens where you know who lives and breathes. Start pedaling Short Round and make a b-line to our next collection.

Short Round, ditch the bike, and fuel the plane. We are headed west again and eighteen hundred miles to the Centennial State and the quaint little town of Northglenn, Colorado. Short Round, make sure to pack the snowshoes and shovel. You just never know.

Maestro, this discovery deserves the loudest drumroll you can muster. Introducing, the once-in-a-Redline Hot Wheels Collectors-lifetime. The spectacular Northglenn, Colorado original, one owner Redline Era Hot Wheels Collection. This is one you most certainly do not want to miss.

The NORTHGLENN, CO Collection
Unearthed: 04.01.2021

No truer words spoken than "Good things come in small packages." Not that this was a "small thing" but it certainly was not one of my larger "Tyrannosaurus Rex" sized finds. The collection totaled forty-eight cars and that was it. Now, please do not take that as "only" forty-eight cars as meaning a hum-drum type of collection, because you will soon find out why my lead in to these four-dozen cars is more of a "Please sit down and take a deep breath" before laying your eyes on what you are about to see.

I received a completed Inquiry form from my website's Contact Page that basically asked if I was interested in seeing this gentleman's collection. I, of course, answered in the affirmative and followed up with an email expressing this. When emailing an owner of what could be a potential find, I am always specific with my directions of where and how to send high-definition pictures of the cars to me. Initially, I instruct the owner of the collection to send me a few overhead group shots of the cars, especially if they are still housed in their original cases. This seems to be the quickest and easiest first step in the process and most comply within a day or two. Just to reiterate, text messaging or emailing are the two options I present, with text messaging being the most widely used of the two.

Almost instantaneously, my phone began dinging as each picture was being texted to me. I just sat down to dinner with my family, so I had to silence my phone. Phones are not permitted during family dinner time at the Youngs, and I am certainly not above the law. This has happened to me before, countless times so I was kind of used to it. I finally finished my dinner and picked up my phone to see if the collection was going to be a home run or just a bunt single. You never know in this realm just what is going to appear on that little screen in front of you.

I have one of the more recent iPhone models with two cameras on it and I can tell you that the resolution of the pictures I take is unbelievable. When I laid my eyes on the dozens of pictures the gentleman sent me, I thought to myself, either my eyes just miraculously became twenty years old again or my cell phone was so out of date already. I could not believe the quality of the cars that were popping up, one after another. Every car looked almost to be fakes or reproductions from someone that really did not know what they were doing because he or she made them look way too good. In other words, too good to be true.

The mind-boggling and pristine original childhood collection from the Denver, Colorado territory.

To say that I was a little enthusiastic about this collection is the understatement of the century, forget about the year. I found myself scratching my head questioning whether or not it was actually real. Thirty minutes went by in a flash as I contemplated over each and every picture looking for any signs of reproductions or fakes. I could not find one thing that suggested that the cars were nothing short of authentic. I picked up my phone after scouring over every picture multiple times and called the gentlemen to discuss the cars and dig deep into the provenance on this somewhat confusing collection.

The incredibly factory fresh creamy pink Beatnik Bandit with a white interior as part of the 48-car original collection from Northglenn, CO.

The complete Original 16 from 1968 in blister pack fresh condition.

When asked about the history or provenance of the collection, the gentleman gave a little chuckle and began the journey down memory lane. He started the story talking everything about his uncle and the great relationship they shared. His uncle was responsible for getting him all his Hot Wheels over the years in the sixties and early seventies. When asked if the cars were played with, he chuckled again and gave a resounding "NO" but said they just enjoyed looking at them and having them around. This was the turning point for me as now I understood the lack of any play wear from the pictures sent. When I questioned him about how and where they were stored, he answered "With Love and Kit Gloves." He went on to say that the cars were kept in the house and out of the basement, attic, and garage. In essence, the cars were kept in a temperature-controlled environment for over fifty years. Well, it was all starting to make sense to me now, and the anticipation of owning this breathtaking group of Redline Hot Wheels was growing with each passing minute. We spoke about our parents and growing up during this era of the sixties, and finally ended the call about an hour later. I meet so many interesting people along the way in this hobby, and I try to never miss an opportunity to get to know them better. We seem to share so many similar and interesting experiences and it always takes me back to a much simpler time in my life.

Highlights of the Northglenn, CO collection.

I could not expedite the appraisal any faster of this astonishing collection as I did not want to waste a second and possibly miss the chance of owning it. The entire collection appeared to be "Mint" as a lot of collectors refer to blazingly clean cars. As I have stated, I do not make it common practice to use the word "Mint" when describing the original Hot Wheels since there are always factory flaws. However, if there were ever a time for me to refer to a car, or in this case, an entire collection as "Mint", this was most definitely it!

A rare member of the Spoiler family. The stunning and sticker-less OLIVE Nitty Gritty Kitty.

I finally finished the exhausting appraisal on this remarkable collection of some of the nicest examples of each casting I have ever seen in my thirty year career. This appraisal demanded a lot more time than usual due to the uniqueness of the condition of every car. Factory or blister pack fresh examples of the original Hot Wheels are becoming more and more scarce as time goes on. As we all know, it is just what happens as time goes on. As usual, I reached out to the owner and scheduled a time to discuss the collection at hand. We agreed on talking the following week as he was tied up with a project at work. Trust me when I say that it was a painstakingly long week for me waiting to talk to the owner of this unbelievable set of cars.

The very desirable line of Customs from the first year of production, 1968.

The time and day finally arrived, and the call was placed to the minute. I am rarely late for anything and this was no exception. Normally I will go over all best cars in the best condition but that basically described the entire collection. Even the common castings in common colors were breathtaking. For the first time in my career, I was a bit speechless when discussing a collection. I muddled through every car and finally made it past the starting gate, down the orange track, into the loop de loop, over the jump ramp, and through the finish gate and presented my very generous offer. He was floored and gave that little chuckle of his and told me he would gladly accept my offer. At that exact moment, I think he was as happy as I was, if that is truly humanly possible.

I discussed the process, and he accepted the terms of shipping the collection and how payment would be made. All was good in the land of Redline Hot Wheels. At least in my world it was.

The collection finally arrived a few days later and I could not keep myself from opening it immediately. I normally wait a day or two to post some pictures on my Facebook page and build a little excitement around the official unveiling. This time was different, exceedingly different. Gently yet firmly, I began to cut through the packing tape holding the box together and there was lots of it. I guess the original owner made sure that nothing would get in or out during shipping. The tape was removed, and the flaps of the shipping box was opened, the bright light almost blinded me, and there it was in all its glory. Forty-eight of the most gorgeous Redline Hot Wheels each wrapped in tissue paper just waiting to say hello. Ok, ok, I know I am being a little bit dramatic but come on, this was an incredibly special moment for me as an impassioned Redline Archeologist and my new-found little friends. I am quite sure most of you understand.

The best example of a Custom T Bird in thirty years of diggin' up original Hot Wheels collection, hands down.

The first car to show its ravishing self to me was the Custom T-Bird. In thirty years of searching out original Redline Era Hot Wheels collections I can confidently say that I have never, and I mean never, found one this nice. Not only did it look like it just got painted and fell off the production line at the Mattel factory in Hawthorne, CA in 1967, but it felt new. It is a ridiculously hard thing to describe if you have never experienced one of the original Redlines in this kind of condition, but it actually felt like new to me. Exactly how they felt back when I was a kid in the sixties when I would rip them out of their blister pack and hold them in my hand staring directly at them in total amazement. It instantly took me back over fifty years to 1968. An incredible feeling that I hope to experience again down the road with another collection if I am fortunate enough.

The near perfect Antifreeze Python in all its glory.

From the Custom T-Bird to the Indy Eagle, they just kept coming, one after another, in the most mind-blowing condition I have ever witnessed in my entire collecting career. To this day, when I think about this collection out of Northglenn, Colorado, I smile at the same time my head moves from side to side without me even knowing it. Absolutely one for the Redline Archeology record books.

With this amazing find, there is no need to single out the best of the best as they all qualify. Maestro, I am sorry to do this to you again, but the best drumroll you have ever given please. Ladies and gentlemen it gives me the great honor and privilege to introduce you all to the remarkable and celebrated original, one owner Redline Era Hot Wheels Collection out of Northglenn, Colorado…

1. *Custom Camaro, BLUE with White Interior*
2. *Custom T Bird, BLUE with White Interior*
3. *Custom Cougar, BLUE*
4. *Custom Firebird, RED*
5. *Custom Mustang, RED with White Interior*
6. *Custom Barracuda, AQUA with White Interior*
7. *Custom Eldorado, RED with White Interior*
8. *Custom Fleetside, ORANGE*
9. *Custom Corvette, GREEN*
10. *Custom Volkswagen, ORANGE with White Interior*
11. *Beatnik Bandit, CREAMY PINK with White Interior*
12. *Python, ANTIFREEZE*
13. *Python, BLUE with White Interior*
14. *Hot Heap, RED with White Interior*
15. *Deora, AQUA*
16. *Silhouette, BLUE*
17. *Ford J-Car, LIME YELLOW*
18. *Nitty Gritty Kitty, OLIVE*
19. *TNT Bird, GREEN with White Interior*
20. *Heavy Chevy, GREEN*
21. *King Kuda, AQUA*
22. *Light My Firebird, RED with White Interior*
23. *Boss Hoss Silver Special CLUB CAR*
24. *Custom Charger, RED*
25. *Classic '57-Bird, Blue with White Interior*
26. *Custom AMX, AQUA*
27. *Classic Nomad, PURPLE*
28. *Custom Continental Mk III, AQUA*
29. *Classic '32 Ford Vicky, ROSE PINK with White Interior*
30. *Classic '31 Ford Woody, ORANGE with White Interior*
31. *Classic '36 Ford Coupe, ORANGE*
32. *Police Cruiser*
33. *Mercedes 280sl, GREEN*
34. *Splittin' Image, BLUE with White Interior*
35. *Jack Rabbit Special with White Interior*
36. *Brahbam Repco F1, RED*
37. *Indy Eagle, AQUA*
38. *Lotus Turbine, GREEN*
39. *Shelby Turbine, BLUE*
40. *Lola GT70, GREEN ENAMEL*
41. *Chapparral 2G, BROWN*
42. *Ford Mk IV, RED ENAMEL*
43. *Paddy Wagon*
44. *McClaren M6A, GREEN*
45. *Turbofire, GOLD*
46. *Tri-Baby, MAGENTA*
47. *Twinmill, AQUA*
48. *Torero, RED*

Like I previously stated, I would be remiss to leave even one car out of this collections' ALL-STAR line-up because they were all unparalleled in their own right. So, there you have it, a collection of epic proportions due to its unmatched beauty. I have decided to keep this collection together and put on display for all to enjoy in the hobby. In my humble opinion, this is truly a piece of Mattel history that truly needs to be preserved. I am more than happy to be the life-long steward and protector of this treasure of a Redline Hot Wheels collection.

Let us get a move on it Short Round. There is no time to waste as we are nearing the end of this incredible journey into the world of Redline Archeology. We are again headed back east to the Spirit of America State, Massachusetts. It gives me great honor and the distinct privilege to introduce you all to the Lunenberg, Massachusetts Collection. Founded on April 6th, 2021. Short Round, you and I need some exercise, so strap on your walking shoes as we are headed on a two-thousand-mile hike east. No Short Round, I am not kidding, and I certainly will not let you piggy-back.

The LUNENBERG, MA Collection
Unearthed: 04.06.2021

I received an email in late March 2021 that read "I have a small toolbox full of old Hot Wheels that I found during an estate sale clean-out. Would you be interested in seeing them?" This collection felt different right from the start. I just had this feeling that there was something uniquely unusual or special about this small grouping of cars living in a toolbox of all things for fifty plus years. Afterall, how many Hot Wheels could you actually fit inside a toolbox? I assumed it was not a large number of cars, and my intuition proved me right. The collection only contained a total of twelve cars all from the years 1968 - 1971. Do not ever let yourself be fooled by things that come in small packages. I have learned this lesson many times over in the past thirty years of searching for these precious jewels we call Redline Hot Wheels. Assuming that a collection is too small to waste your time on can be nothing short of foolish in this hobby. I have dug up some of the rarest and most desirable cars in the hobby in what would be considered ridiculously small collections.

I got on the phone with the seller and was a bit surprised to hear a younger gentleman's voice on the other end, but as time went on, I realized that he was an entrepreneur just starting out trying to build a business of his own. I always enjoy talking with fellow entrepreneurs and business men or women as I find them remarkably interesting as risk takers in all types of ventures. I have had many people over the years laugh, chuckle, and shake their collective heads in disbelief at me with my business endeavors, but I, for some reason, take it as a compliment. It is something only a true and seasoned entrepreneur would understand.

I asked the gentleman what the circumstances were that surrounded this mysterious toolbox full of a dozen Redline Hot Wheels. He went on to describe the business he was in and that it was something he stumbled across in the attic of an old estate during a professional clean out. It was also discovered that the toolbox was possibly owned by a former Mattel employee from over fifty years ago. I inquired about the toolbox, but it was already disposed of due to its poor condition. I would have really enjoyed looking through the old toolbox seeing if there was anything else that could have led to a more detailed and thorough provenance of it and all the cars. Oh well, you cannot win them all.

The gentleman decided that the email route was the best way for him to send pictures of the cars to me, so he stated that he would get them to me over the next few days. I was basically sitting on the edge of my seat in anticipation of what my instincts were telling me was a potentially big score. Dreaming of prototypes, early production models, and anything else that might have never been seen in the hobby was what was running through my Redline centric mind at the time while I continued to wait patiently. The day finally came, and the email notification popped up on my phone, and we were off to the orange track races. I opened the first file, and it was the strangest looking Continental Mk III I had ever laid eyes on. I had to zoom in and out a few times, trying to wrap my mind around what was in front of my eyes on the iPhone screen. The car was as clean an example of a Continental Mk III as I have ever come across, but there was one not so subtle difference. The roof and all four pillars appeared to be painted flat black and looked to be professionally done at the Mattel factory in 1970. The roof was reminiscent of the flat black roofs of cars like the Custom Fleetside, Python, The Demon, Rolls Royce Silver Shadow, Maserati Mistral, Custom Cougar, Custom Eldorado, Custom T-Bird, Classic '31 Ford Woody, Classic '32 Ford Vicky, and Classic '36 Ford Coupe. Same color, same texture, same look, and same exact feel but all four pillars were painted as well. Again, it appeared to come right off the factory line in every respect. The nay-sayers seem to come out of the woodwork when a car like this pops up in an original collection of Redline Hot Wheels that I discover in what I call the "Wild." They all have their opinions on why it is not a rare find. They are kind of like judge, jury, and executioner all wrapped up into one. This scenario has happened to me at least a dozen times over the years, and I do respect other knowledgeable collector's opinions, but I do take them with a grain of salt. The ORANGE Classic Cord that I discovered as part of the Tacony, Pennsylvania collection years ago and more recently the RED Classic '31 Ford Woody that surfaced as part of the Red Oak, Iowa collection are just two examples of this. They were both dismissed by some in the hobby as not being early production, test cars, nor prototypes. I guess it is what keeps us all engaged in this wonderful, fun, and exciting hobby that we all hold near and dear to our hearts.

The one of one Continental Mk III with a painted black roof that has never been seen in the hobby until now.

As I was scrolling through all the pictures of each car contained within the collection, I noticed another car that raised an eyebrow or two. It was the unstickered version of the 1973 OLDS 442 Police Cruiser. The paint on the car was so clean and deep in texture that it deserved a closer look. It was virtually flawless as well. I have only come across this casting with the proverbial "Police" sticker that was always factory applied to it on both sides, but this one had no evidence of it ever being applied. I examined the car closely and found zero evidence of any sticker residue left behind. The car was as clean as you can possibly imagine. Taking this into consideration and upon further inspection, the car appeared to have been pulled from the line prior to the stickers being applied or may have been a test car of some sorts. We may never know. I do have to admit that I have always preferred any OLDS 442 casting to be sticker-less. For this reason, this one will certainly have a spot reserved in my personal collection.

The 1973 version of the OLDS 442 Police Cruiser minus its factory applied stickers on both doors.

Good things do come in small toolboxes after all.

    The other cars found in the collection were all in near mint to factory fresh condition as well. Even though there were only a dozen cars in total in this complex collection, it took me a tremendous amount of time and effort to properly appraise the cars. I painstakingly had to cross reference some of the pieces with many recent auction sales and bounce some of the cars off fellow trusted, experienced, and knowledgeable Redline Hot Wheels collectors to get their professional opinions on the cars' authenticity. Like I have said before, I take every opinion with a huge grain of salt.

    I finally was confident in my appraisal and presented it and my offer to the young gentleman. He was stunned and floored by my offer. He told me that he had shopped the collection locally and was told by one potential buyer and collector that he basically had nothing there and only offered him a hundred dollars. I am going to reserve comment at this time, and I think you all already know what I would say anyway at this juncture. Needless to say, my offer was graciously accepted by the gentlemen and my check and his cars passed each other in the USPS mail as both arrived at their respective destinations the same exact day. I love it when a plan comes together.

The cars arrived on Tuesday April 6th, 2021 and I was stoked to get an up-close look at each car. Each car, due to the collection's unique provenance deserved a detailed and thorough going over. Upon inspection of each car, nothing really stood out except for what I already knew about this collection. The Continental Mk III did have a flat black professionally looking factory paint job of its roof and four pillars and the 1973 OLDS 442 Police Cruiser was absolutely spotless and appeared to have multiple layers of the most beautiful, deep, and rich white enamel paint I have ever seen in this casting or any of the enamels produced by Mattel. Will we ever know the truth about this collection or the two cars in question as to whether they are prototypes or not? Who knows, but what I do know is that this small find out of Lunenberg, Massachusetts is staying put until I do.

Without further ado, I want to introduce the entire cast from the mysterious attic find out of Lunenberg, Massachusetts. A legendary, original Redline Era Hot Wheels collection in its own right.

1. **Continental Mk III, MAGENTA with Painted Black Roof + Pillars**
2. **OLDS 442 1973 Police Cruiser, Sticker-less**
3. **Custom Cougar, ORANGE with White Interior**
4. **Classic Cord, LITE GREEN**
5. **Bye-Focal, AQUA**
6. **Open Fire, MAGENTA**
7. **Custom Camaro, BLUE**
8. **Custom Charger, AQUA**
9. **Custom Fleetside, AQUA**
10. **Police Cruiser**
11. **Mercedes 280sl, AQUA**
12. **Classic '31 Ford Woody, RED with White Interior**

Every car, due to the collections somewhat inexplicable and unexplained provenance, needs a much closer look from not only me, but from other experienced and accomplished collectors. The Spirit of America state came through in a big way for this Redline fanatic.

Hey Short Round, where were you? You look like you just woke up. Poor little guy's legs were so tired from our two-thousand-mile hike. I guess we have successfully reached the end of the road on our greatest discoveries of the last three years. Who knows what the next three years will bring in the Redline Archeology world, but I know that I cannot wait to see what collections surface next.

Chapter 9
The Final Tally

If I would have kept every car and collection that I have unearthed in my thirty-year career in the Redline Hot Wheels hobby, I would seriously and literally need two ten-thousand square foot warehouses to store everything. I am not kidding in the least. A lot of collectors think that I have this massive Redline Hot Wheels collection, but in essence, I only keep what I like and can display, and the cars in the absolute nicest condition, which totals a very modest three hundred cars and some accessories.

My very modest collection of all the cars that I love, which is all the Redlines.

I have estimated over the last thirty years, just how many total cars and collections that I have dug up out of individuals' attics, basements, garages, storage facilities, and homes. The conservative total to date, including every car as of the writing of this book, sits at approximately twenty-seven thousand cars and counting. An average collection that I discover is typically between fifty to seventy-two cars. If you do the math, that equates to approximately four hundred and fifty collections of Redline Era Hot Wheels. If I were to keep this pace, I should eclipse thirty thousand cars and five hundred collections by the end of the year 2024. A lofty goal but a very attainable one at the rate I am going. Each year, for the last thirty years, my car and collection total has consistently increased over time. I will have to make a safe assumption that this will continue, and my goals will be not only attained, but surpassed. Chances are, that if you have been in this hobby long enough, you probably have a car or multiple cars that initially passed through my dusty hands. You may even see them mentioned and or pictured in one of my two books and other collector's guides throughout the hobby. How cool is that!

Some of my favorite things Mattel created as part of the Hot Wheels amazing line up, the Rrumblers.

Passionate Hot Wheels collectors reach out to me all the time asking whether I feel that the ability to find these rare one owner original Redline Era Hot Wheels collections are drying up. This question has been posed to me almost since the beginning, way back in 1992. My answer is that I have and continue to stand by the belief that I am the perfect example of why the Redline Era Hot Wheels collections are still out there just waiting to be discovered and brought to light. It does take a lot of work, time, ingenuity, and most importantly, perseverance to dig up these special cars and collections, but it can be done. I cannot stress how important it truly is to never take any situation for granted, and never, and I mean never, miss an opportunity to get the word out to anyone and everyone, that you are "the guy" or "gal" that buys the original Redline Era Hot Wheels. It is a fairly easy topic to work into most conversations, but you will just need some practice to fine tune it.

The rarest collector buttons in the hobby, the plastic and earlier metal OLDS 442.

My quest for what I and a lot of others believe to be the greatest and most ingenious car toy line ever created, Redline Era Hot Wheels, has only begun. Searching the fifty states and beyond is a task that I enjoy and am willing to take on. The ride along the way has its ups and downs, and at times you will get discouraged thinking that you may have run out of rope or come upon the end of the road. Do not despair, as I know, when it rains it certainly pours Redlines. You just must persevere through the droughts and dry spells. The feeling of opening the orange plastic Flat Cases, Rally Wheel Cases, or Stack Cases that have not been unlatched for decades, is something that never diminishes over time and truly keeps me motivated knowing the next great find is just around the orange track half curve. The smell of the original Redline Hot Wheels and all the accessories is a very distinct one and one that all who grew up during this special time during the sixties knows all too well. It always proves to be a memory jogger for this guy, taking that first whiff of a new unearthed collection. I can see a lot of you right now nodding your collective heads in agreement with that big grin plastered across your face.

Chapter 10
The BEST of the BEST Discoveries

Over the thirty-year span of my collecting career, I have brought to light and unearthed some of the most remarkable and incredibly rare cars the hobby has ever seen. From the ORANGE Classic Cord to the carded ORANGE King Kuda with a Black Roof and White Interior, to the BLUE Power Pad and PURPLE Short Order, there have been way too many to list. The last three years have brought forth some cars that would rival the four aforementioned pieces and were just as phenomenal. I have decided to compile a list of the "TOP 25" cars discovered in the last three years by yours truly. All the cars ranked and listed are just a small piece of each original collection's entirety. Grab your favorite beverage, sit back, and let me tell you a story about some incredible and rarely if ever seen Redline Era Hot Wheels.

Some of the nicest condition and rarest cars in the Redline hobby.

This was a difficult and very tough list for me to put together as I genuinely appreciate every Hot Wheels casting from the Redline Era of 1968 – 1977. However, my favorite years of production were 1968 – 1972, the Spectraflame era. So, you can see that it is extremely difficult for me to pick my "TOP 25" favorites from all the amazing designs that were put forth during the first five years of Hot Wheels at Mattel. Looking back over the last three years of discoveries, I have painstakingly constructed a list of what I feel were my greatest and most memorable, rare, and incredible finds. In other words, the BEST of the BEST in the factory fresh condition as well. So here we go with my "TOP 25" Redlines of the past three years found in original, one owner Redline Era Hot Wheels collections... Enjoy! I certainly know I did!!

1. *Custom Camaro, BROWN*
2. *Classic '31 Ford Woody, RED Prototype*
3. *Custom Charger, ORANGE*
4. *Custom Barracuda, ORANGE with White Interior*
5. *Classic '36 Ford Coupe, PURPLE with White Interior + Purple Rumble Seat, Prototype*
6. *Rolls Royce Silver Shadow, PURPLE*
7. *Sidekick, AQUA*
8. *Mighty Maverick, HOT PINK, No Stripes, Early production release*
9. *Custom Barracuda, ICE BLUE with White Interior*
10. *Mantis, ORANGE with White Interior*
11. *Custom Volkswagen, ICE BLUE with White Interior*
12. *Custom Cougar, ORANGE with White Interior*
13. *Custom Cougar, OLIVE with Black Roof + White Interior*
14. *Continental Mk III, MAGENTA with Black Roof + Pillars, Prototype, 1 of 1*
15. *Beatnik Bandit, HOT PINK*
16. *Volkswagen Beach Bomb, YELLOW with White Interior*
17. *Boss Hoss, OLIVE with Black Roof + White Interior*
18. *Tow Truck, HOT PINK with White Interior*
19. *Cockney Cab, HOT PINK*
20. *Evil Weevil, AQUA with White Interior*
21. *OLDS 442, LITE BLUE*
22. *Deora, RED*
23. *Custom Eldorado, HOT PINK*
24. *Brabham Repco F-1, RED with White Interior*
25. *Sky Show Fleetside, PURPLE*

Rolls Royce Silver Shadow in the exceedingly rare color of PURPLE along with the very mysterious Continental Mk III with the Black painted roof and pillars.

There are many more in all the collections that I have discovered over the last thirty-six months that you certainly could make a case for to be on this list, but these were the "TOP 25" out of over four thousand Redline Hot Wheels that were unearthed by me that have risen to the top of the Tune-Up Tower per se. Some collectors may challenge some of the cars' authenticity, which is not unexpected due to their extreme rarity or never being heard of or seen before. It is the main reason why I never say never in this fascinating hobby of ours. Just when you thought a certain casting was not produced in a certain color, "BANG", next thing you know, one shows its incredibly rare and beautiful self in an original collection that I unearth. This is just another reason why I always try to gather the provenance, and as much additional information as possible about the original owner and entire collection as I possibly can. Some cars on this list, we may never know the absolute truth about its origins, but we must always consider the provenance and other seasoned and scholarly collectors' opinions. I tend to keep an open mind in this hobby and listen to everyone's opinions, including relying on my own experience. One thing that this wonderful hobby has taught me over the years is to never think you know everything about every car ever produced by Mattel during the Redline Era. I learn something new almost every day that I spend in this hobby and that is just another reason I enjoy the hobby so much. I know that there is so much more to learn about this wonderful toy car line, and I cannot wait!

CHAPTER 11

The REDLINE ARCHEOLOGY Personal Collection

With all the tens of thousands of cars and hundreds of original, one owner collections of the Redline Era Hot Wheels that I unearth, you would think that I have warehouses full of them. This is about as far from reality as it gets for me. As I have stated, I only keep a few hundred of my favorite cars in my favorite colors and in the absolute best condition. The most determining factor whether a car makes it into my personal collection is condition. Condition, Condition, Condition as in the words of you know who. A car's individual rarity and desirability to collectors is defined in many ways by each individual collector. I define rarity based on an individual car's overall condition. If the car is in what appears at times to be what we call in the hobby as the "Over-Chrome" look, then to me, it is absolutely and fundamentally rare. Collectors like to argue this point with me at times, but I have brought a lot of passionate Redline collectors to my side of the fence over the years. In my most humble opinion, condition determines value every time and all the time. Period, and exclamation point! A common casting in a common color may have significantly more value if it is truly virtually flawless in my opinion. Another trend I have noticed over three decades of collecting Redlines is that the factory fresh cars with little or no wear not only hold their values over time, but have always increased in value over time, every time.

A few examples of cars with virtually zero flaws which make them a rarity in the hobby.

I understand totally that I do have a huge advantage of being able to cherry pick only the best and brightest out of each collection that I discover, but I also know that I am also limited to the amount of display space in my cases. This is where all the other Redline collectors benefit as I try to get them in the hands of those that deeply appreciate these precious treasures and display them for the world to see. Like I stated earlier, there is a remarkably high statistical probability that you, as a Redline collector, own one or multiples of cars that I unearthed over the past three decades. I hear it all the time and sometimes from individuals I have never met. Always a satisfying and proud moment for me to know that I have contributed to someone else's happiness in the hobby.

My humble collection of Redlines from the past thirty years.

Black Interior OLDS 442 Prototype, GOLD Chrome Porsche 911 Salesman Car, Prototype LITE BLUE Paddy Wagon, along with other beautiful examples of some of the rarest and most desirable cars in the hobby today.

Rarely do I ever treat myself by purchasing a car online or from another Redline collector. For me, when the urge hits to add another piece to my collection that has not shown itself in thirty years of searching, "BANG", there it is, right in front of me in an original collection that I just unearthed. It is a very strange thing, but it has absolutely happened to me on more than one occasion. Patience is absolutely a virtue in this hobby if you can wait long enough for a car to show up in a collection that you may be fortunate to buy. I have literally waited decades for a certain casting in a certain color to show up in a collection and continue to do so for a few cars I still hold out hope for. I waited twenty-six years for a PURPLE Short Order, my favorite casting in my favorite color, to show its elusive self when it finally surfaced in an original, one owner Redline Era Hot Wheels collection out of the Centennial State in a town called Windsor, Colorado. It also happened to be one of the cleanest cars in the entire collection to boot. I was stunned as the pictures that were originally sent to me by the owner depicted the car as BLUE. Talk about a pleasant surprise for tired eyes. A car that will never leave my showcase. You can take that to the bank in a LITE GREEN Short Order. Afterall, I cannot risk scratching the PURPLE one, right? I knew you would agree.

Seeing if the car in hand will join the chosen few.

My most prized Redline Hot Wheel of all time, the coveted PURPLE Short Order.

So, there you have it, a peek into my unique and crazy world of searching out the Redline Era Hot Wheels collections that have been stored away for decades. Many of my friends and family members have seen my collection firsthand, and something odd happens every time someone from my age group ventures into my Redline themed Hot Wheels office. They instantly seem to get mesmerized and a smile, from ear to ear immediately appears. Words and phrases are mumbled like "Oh my, I had that car when I was a kid, and that one and that one", "That is the Red Baron right?" "Wow, that was my favorite car", "Where did you get all these Hot Wheels?", "This is unbelievable", "I love it", "I remember the orange track, loop de loop, and purple clamps", "We would play with our Hot Wheels for hours", "I wish I still had my old Hot Wheels", "I loved my Hot Wheels", and many more comments and gasps, and certainly too many to list.

The other odd thing that happens almost every time someone steps foot into my office is that I seem to have a hard time getting them out. I would estimate that the typical dinner guest explores my collection for at least fifteen to thirty minutes on average. I absolutely love sharing my collection and all the wonderful stories from my experiences as a child of the sixties and as an adult collector, and other's experiences growing up with the greatest toy car line every produced, Hot Wheels.

CHAPTER 12

The Beginning

I know, I know, what a strange name for the final chapter to my book. I totally get it, but I found this title to be so apropos for the last chapter of this incredibly special book. This hobby, or as my friend Jacuveline calls it, "Jobby", will always encompass a part of my life, and will continue to hold a special place in my heart. My burning desire to become an archaeologist from my earliest years and digging up the Parkview Elementary School playground looking for any old stuff, which was just down the block from my childhood home on Hillcrest Road in the special town of Stratford, New Jersey, continues in me just as strong now as it was in the sixties.

No truer words have been spoken than those of Kenny Chesney's 2007 Hit Song "Don't Blink." The last thirty years have gone by in a flash, and it feels like I am only beginning this journey into the Redline World of Archeology. Sounds crazy, but it really tells you just how much I enjoy doing what I do; diggin' up the original Redline Era Hot Wheels collections. I consider myself blessed in so many ways, and this is just one of them.

One of the recent discoveries unearthed by the "Indiana Jones" of Redline Collecting.

Our beloved hobby is as strong now as I have ever witnessed over the past three decades of hunting down Redlines, and only appears to be gaining strength. Yes, we are all getting older, but the fever seems to be growing amongst us older guys and gals, and there also seems to be more and more passionate, younger collectors getting onboard recently as well. I have also witnessed an influx of collectors from my generation at a startling rate. It has always been obvious to me that people want to go back and capture a small slice of their childhoods, and the Redline Era Hot Wheels certainly fills that void in so many wonderful and exciting ways. The future of the hobby is extremely bright, and I hope I can continue to get all the greatest Redlines in impassioned collector's hands as I have been doing all along. It is a great feeling to hear someone say, "Hey, I have some of the cars you discovered in my collection, and I actually recognized them talked about and pictured in your first book." This type of comment really gives me a great sense of accomplishment and a feeling of contributing to this wonderful hobby of ours. Every new collection that I discover only motivates me even more to find the next great one and the next one and so on. It is like hitting a walk off grand slam in the bottom of the ninth inning when your team is down three runs. A feeling every true passionate Redline collector deserves to experience at least once in their careers.

The spoils of the Hunt + Capture for one of the most unique Redline Hot Wheels collectors in the world.

There will always be those, in any hobby, that can and will leave a negative mark. We need to put those people and their efforts in our rear views and keep moving this hobby forward. Do not ever look back, keep your eyes on the orange track and loop de loop in front of you, and you will find yourself crossing through that finish gate in first place every time. I learned this lesson a long time ago and it has sustained me throughout this last thirty years while enjoying every moment, and each beautiful Redline Hot Wheel car and Redline Hot Wheels collection along the way.

I always try to set a positive and good example in life, and this hobby is certainly no exception to the rule. We all need to respect each other's style of collecting and support it in any way we can as a community. Giving to others out of the kindness of your heart is the greatest and most rewarding feeling in the world. Do not ever hesitate to RAOK (Random Act of Kindness) or donate a car or cars to a fellow collector or their families. Being generous in this hobby speaks volumes to your character and is something we all need to do more of in support of not only each other, but for the hobby. Remember, an individual's character is best tested when it is up against it. You will be quite astounded by what you eventually get back tenfold.

Afterall, I consider this next chapter of my collector life as my starting gate, or what I like to otherwise refer to as "The Beginning." The Dig Continues…..

Another successful capture for the Redline Archeologist!

To All Readers,

I just wanted to thank each and every one of you for purchasing and reading this, my second book in the REDLINE ARCHEOLOGY series. I hope you all enjoyed reading it as much as I enjoyed living it! There is much more to come in the world of Redline Hot Wheels and REDLINE ARCHEOLOGY. Who knows what amazing finds are just around the corner. My quest for the original Redlines continues just as strong today as was my love for Hot Wheels way back in 1968.

If you have any of your beloved Hot Wheels from the production years 1967 – 1976 and are looking to sell, please feel free to reach out to me on my cell phone @ 856.912.2463 or my email @ Bob@GeeseChasers.com

Again, thank you for your continued support and love of Hot Wheels.

Yours in the Hunt & Capture,

Bob "Indy" Young

www.ingramcontent.com/pod-product-compliance
Lightning Source LLC
Chambersburg PA
CBHW041402020526
44115CB00036B/6